NEED to KNOW

Key facts at your fingertips

HIGHER PE

John Millar

Janice Smith

HODDER
GIBSON
AN HACHETTE UK COMPANY

Although every effort has been made to ensure that website addresses are correct at time of going to press, Hodder Gibson cannot be held responsible for the content of any website mentioned in this book. It is sometimes possible to find a relocated web page by typing in the address of the home page for a website in the URL window of your browser.

Orders: please contact Bookpoint Ltd, 130 Park Drive, Milton Park, Abingdon, Oxon OX14 4SE. Telephone: (44) 01235 827827. Fax: (44) 01235 400454. Email education@bookpoint.co.uk. Lines are open from 9 a.m. to 5 p.m., Monday to Friday, with a 24-hour message answering service. Visit our website at www. hoddereducation. co.uk. If you have queries or questions that aren't about an order, you can contact us at hoddergibson@hodder.co.uk

© John Millar and Janice Smith 2019

First published in 2019 by
Hodder Gibson, an imprint of Hodder Education
An Hachette UK Company
211 St Vincent Street
Glasgow, G2 5QY

Impression number 5 4 3

Year   2023 2022 2021 2020

Illustrations by Aptara, Inc.
Typeset by Aptara, Inc.
Printed in Spain

A catalogue record for this title is available from the British Library.

ISBN: 978 1 5104 5118 6

Hachette UK's policy is to use papers that are natural, renewable and recyclable products and made from wood grown in well-managed forests and other controlled sources. The logging and manufacturing processes are expected to conform to the environmental regulations of the country of origin.

Contents

Contents

Getting the most from this book

This *Need to Know* guide is designed to help you throughout your course as a companion to your learning and a revision aid in the months or weeks leading up to the final exams.

The following features in each section will help you get the most from the book.

You need to know

Each topic begins with a list summarising what you 'need to know' in this topic for the exam.

Exam tips

Key knowledge you need to demonstrate in the exam, tips on exam technique, common misconceptions to avoid and important things to remember.

Key terms

Definitions of highlighted terms in the text to make sure you know the essential terminology for your subject.

Do you know?

Questions at the end of each topic to test you on some of its key points. Check your answers here: www.hoddereducation.co.uk/ needtoknow/answers

End of section questions

Questions at the end of each main section of the book to test your knowledge of the specification area covered. Check your answers here: www.hoddereducation.co.uk/needtoknow/answers

Introduction

Higher PE

The Higher PE course assessment consists of:

- two separate performances in a challenging context
- an exam, which will be based on four factors – mental, emotional, social and physical – structured as follows:

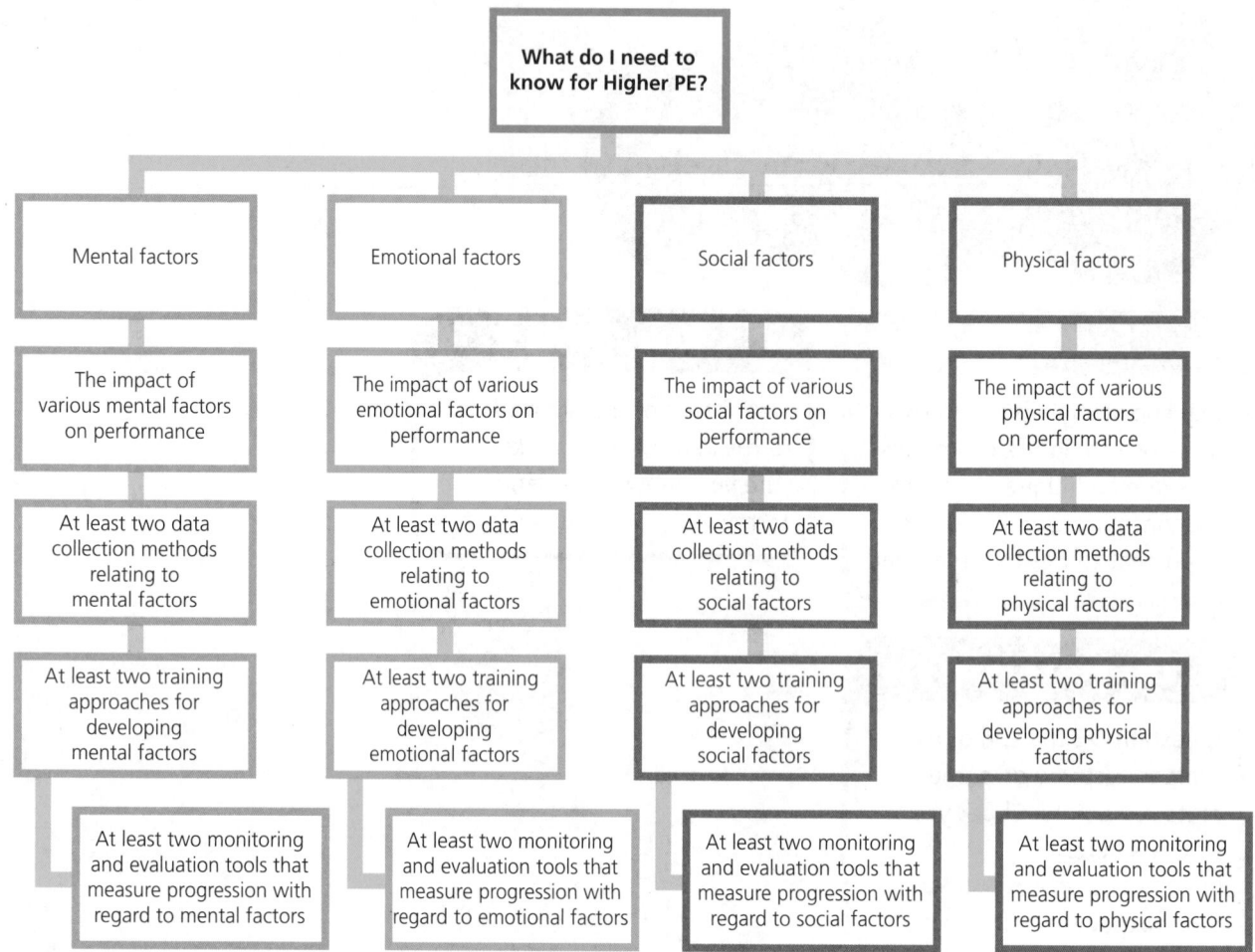

Your performances count towards 50% of the course award. The exam counts towards the other 50% of the course award.

Performance

The following table shows an overview of the criteria that will be used to assess your two performances.

How each of your two performances is assessed

Criteria	Marks
Repertoire of skills	7
Control and fluency	7
Effective decision making	7
Using and applying well established composition, tactics and roles safely and effectively	7
Extent to which rules and regulations are followed and etiquette is displayed (including working with others)	1
Extent to which emotions are controlled on the day of the performance	1
Total marks	**30**

Exam

SQA Higher PE exam structure

Exam structure	Marks
Section 1	32
Covers all four factors (mental, emotional, social and physical) Students will be expected to have knowledge of the following aspects: ■ factors impacting on performance ■ data collection ■ approaches used to develop performance ■ methods for monitoring and evaluating	
Section 2	6–10
Personal development plans on two different factors Must be over a minimum of three sessions	
Section 3	8–12
Scenario could come in the form of a table, text, image or graph Scenario will look for students to solve a performance problem or challenge	

Each aspect of the course should be applied across all four factors:

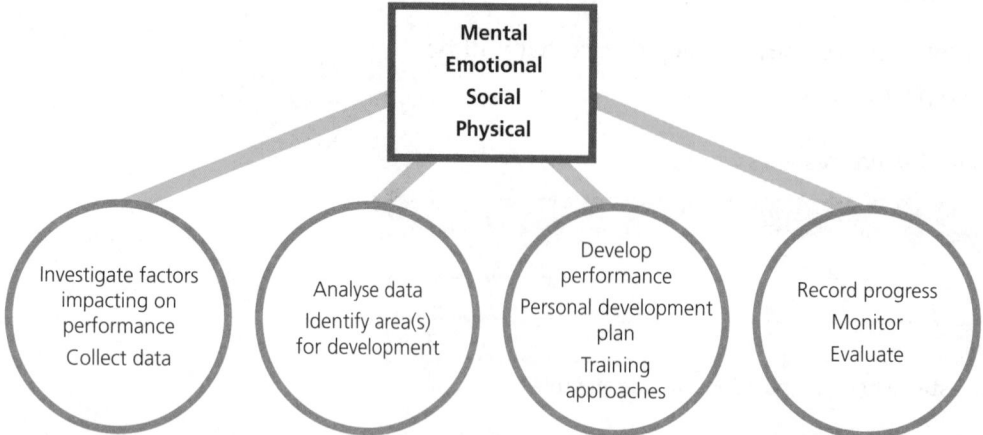

Command words

There are five command words that you need to be aware of in the Higher PE exam. You need to have an in-depth understanding of each one to be able to apply your knowledge of the course appropriately.

Identify

If you are asked to identify you need to be able to:

- Recall key points of knowledge
- Give points that reflect the number of marks available. For example, if one mark is available you need to be able to give one correct point.

Describe

If you are asked to describe, you need to be able to give details about:

- what something looks like
- how something was carried out
- where it was carried out
- when it was carried out

Analyse

If you are asked to analyse, you need to be able to:

- look beyond the explanation and give another reason why
- break down the information to look in more detail

Explain

If you are asked to explain, you need to be able to give details about:

- why something is the way it is
- why you have used something
- why a particular method/approach is appropriate
- why a factor impacts on performance

Evaluate

If you are asked to evaluate, you need to be able to:

- make a judgement and give the value of it when evaluating performance or the personal development plan
- if appropriate, provide quantifiable data to back up what you are saying.

Identify

- **Identify one method you used to gather information on the physical factor.**
- General observation schedule
- Movement analysis sheet
- Bleep test
- Standardised fitness tests
- T15 swim test

Describe

- **Describe one method you used to gather information on the physical factor.**
- I collected data by completing a scatter graph on a half court.
- My partner fed me 10 shuttles high and deep to the back of the court.
- I returned the shuttles one after the other using an overhead clear.
- I then recorded where the shuttles landed using my scatter graph.

Explain

- **Explain one method you used to gather information on the physical factor.**
- I used the scatter graph to collect information on my performance in the physical factor. I chose this method because I could record my scores on my scatter graph. This is good because it allows me to keep my initial results as a performance record which I can later use to compare with future retests which allows me to check for any improvements.

Analyse

- **Analyse one method you used to gather information on the physical factor.**
- The scatter graph was very easy to understand and simple to carry out. Due to the simplicity of the method, I didn't make any mistakes when carrying it out. This meant that the results I gained from it were reliable. Similarly, as it was simple to carry out, it did not take me long to complete. This means that I did not waste time gathering the data and more time could be spent on developing my identified weaknesses.

Evaluate

- **Evaluate one method you used to gather information on the physical factor.**
- The scatter graph was very easy to understand. This allows a wide range of people to use it from beginners to more experienced performers – without taking too much time to explain it.
- As the results are laid out in a quantitative way it is very straightforward to set achievable targets. If a performer lands 4/10 clears in the court then they can set an achievable target of improving this to 6/10 by the end of the PDP.

1 Mental factors

1.1 Factors impacting on performance

You need to know

- definitions of mental factors (examples are given for mental toughness, decision making, level of arousal)
- how each mental factor might affect performance negatively
- how each mental factor might affect performance positively

Mental toughness

Mental toughness is a measure of individual resilience and confidence that can predict success in sport. It involves the following attributes:

- Reboundability – being able to bounce back from setbacks and mistakes. Dwelling on mistakes can lead to a negative performance.
- Handling pressure – being able to stay calm when under pressure. If you get too nervous, your muscles can tighten which will lead to a negative performance.
- Concentration – being able to focus on what is important and block out any distractions. Lack of concentration can lead to mistakes.
- Motivation – being able to push yourself to achieve your goals. Performers can either be intrinsically or extrinsically motivated.
- Confidence – having belief in yourself that you can be successful and not be shaken by setbacks and failures.

You can use the FACI structure to think about mental toughness. Here are two examples:

F	Mental (mental toughness)
A	Swimming
C	I need good mental toughness in swimming. For example, I was very anxious before the race started and struggled to block out the noise of the crowd. Therefore, when the whistle went I was unable to react quickly.
I	As I was unable to react quickly to the whistle, I was slow off the blocks, which meant I was behind my competitors. I was unable to close the gap from there and did not win the race.

Key term

Mental toughness The ability to cope with pressure in demanding situations in order to perform at the highest level.

Exam tip

Use the acronym FACI to structure your answers. Your answer must have all four points to access 1 mark:

F   Factor – name the factor and approach involved

A   Activity – name the activity

C   Context – this must link to the performance

I   Impact – the positive or negative impact

F	Mental (mental toughness)
A	Gymnastics
C	During my gymnastics routine, I slipped and fell off the beam. I was able to get straight back on and continue with the rest of my routine without thinking about my mistake.
I	As I was able to recover immediately from my mistake and continue my routine till the end without any more mistakes, I was only deducted marks once.

Decision making

- Whenever you are in a challenging performance context, you will be expected to make decisions.
- The decisions you make will have either a positive or a negative impact on performance.
- Some decisions can be made before a performance/game while others are made in the moment.
- A decision tree can allow you to think about when to make decisions in sporting contexts (Figure 1 shows some examples).

> **Key term**
>
> Decision making The ability to choose the best option available to you. This is based on what is happening around you and can improve and become more automatic with experience.

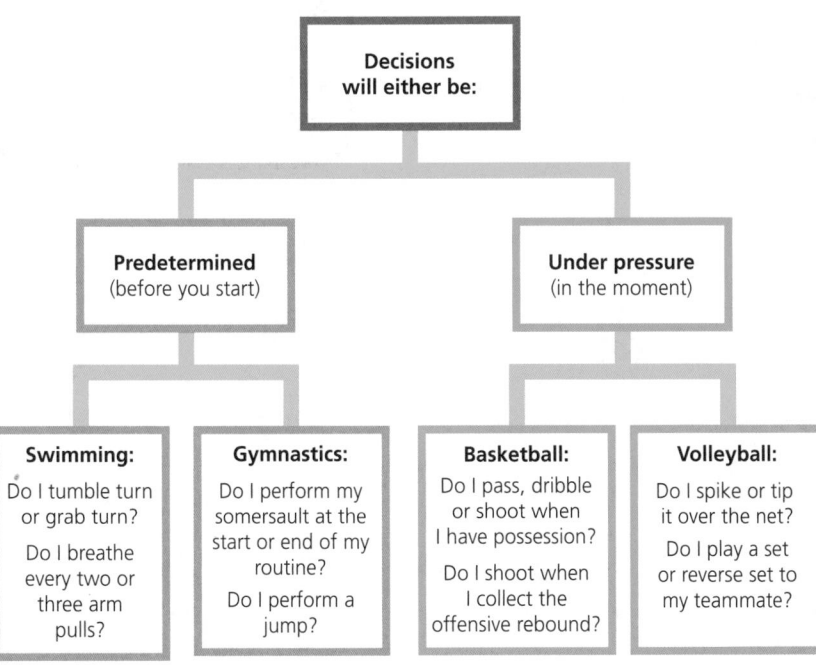

Figure 1 A decision tree

You can use the FACI structure to think about decision making. Here are two examples:

F	Mental (decision making)
A	Football
C	My decision making negatively impacted my performance in football when I made the wrong decision in an attacking 2v1 situation. Despite noticing my teammate in space, I decided to dribble past the defender to make more space for myself to shoot.
I	This led to my being tackled by an opponent and our attack breaking down. From there the opposition was able to start their own attack towards our goal.

F	Mental (decision making)
A	Dance
C	I decided to choreograph and perform a double pirouette in my final performance instead of a single. I was able to complete the double pirouette effectively without falling out of it.
I	I was awarded more marks for the double pirouette, as this is a skill with a higher degree of difficulty.

Level of arousal

- Success in sport can often be determined by a performer's level of arousal.
- To achieve successful outcomes in sport, performers need to be able to reach and maintain the right level of arousal.
- This is primarily because both too little (under-arousal) and too much (over-arousal) can have negative impacts on performance (Figure 2).

Key term

Arousal An energised mental state of alertness and preparedness for an activity.

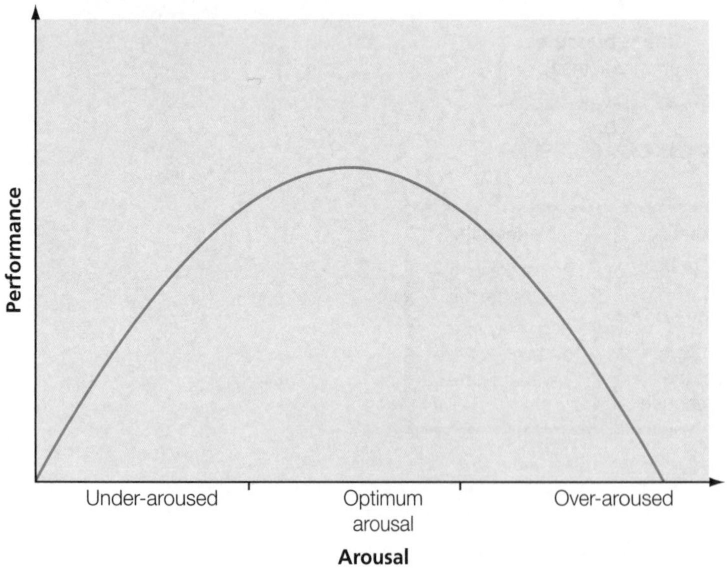

Figure 2 Optimal arousal

Your level of arousal can fluctuate depending on the situation you are placed in. Table 1 shows some examples of what can happen when you are in a specific state of arousal.

Table 1 Levels of arousal

Level of arousal	What can happen?
Over-aroused	▪ Nervousness and a surge of adrenalin can negatively impact performance, resulting in unpredictable behaviour. ▪ Fear and anxiety can consume an individual, resulting in a loss of timing, balance, fluency and skill success. ▪ Over stimulation results in a performer missing important cues/stimuli in a game. This will impact the information processing system and impair judgements and decisions. ▪ A performer may get angry or distracted if over-aroused.
Optimal arousal	▪ The performer operates at their very best. ▪ Emotional, physical and mental arousal are at their peak. ▪ Sufficient adrenalin creates excitement but maintains composure. ▪ The cognitive processes are at their most productive.
Under-aroused	▪ Performers may be over relaxed and not hyped up enough for an event. This is often caused by over confidence. ▪ Under-arousal causes lapses in concentration, resulting in errors. Training can suffer when a person is in this mental state because motivation is reduced.

Level of arousal can be affected by the factors shown in Figure 3.

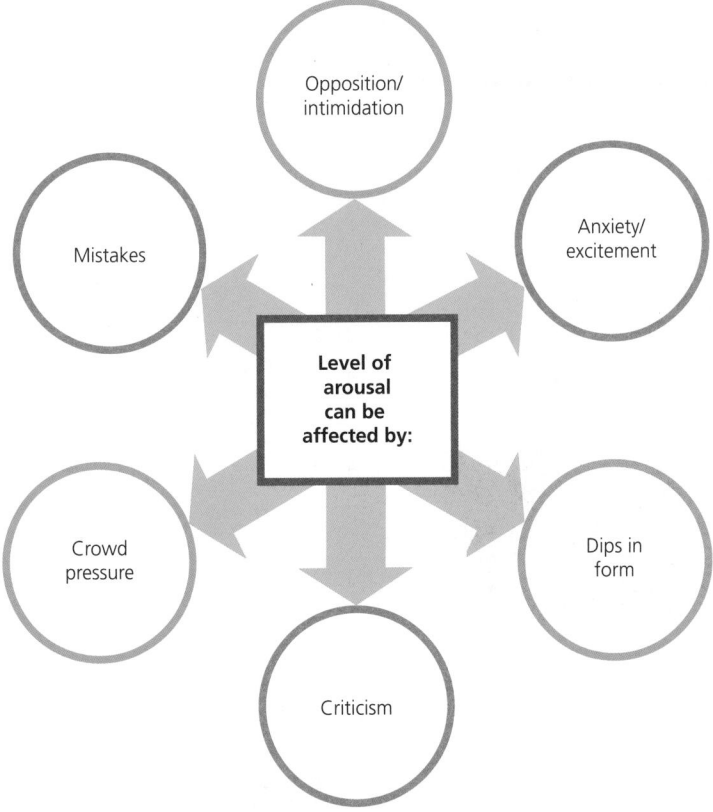

Figure 3 Factors impacting level of arousal

You can use the FACI structure to think about level of arousal.
Here are two examples:

F	Mental (level of arousal)
A	100 m sprint
C	I was so nervous/anxious in the lead-up to my final race that I was experiencing muscle tension. When the race started, I was unable to run as fast and fluently as I had in training.
I	I was over-aroused and this ultimately slowed me down. I was unable to catch my competitors and I lost the race.

F	Mental (level of arousal)
A	Volleyball
C	My low level of arousal meant I was not motivated to do my best in the game. For example, when my opponent spiked the ball, I could have dived to pick it up, but did not.
I	This resulted in my team losing the point because the ball hit the floor.

Do you know?

1 Describe how mental factors might influence a performer who lacks mental toughness in a team game.

2 Explain the impact of a performer being under-aroused when in a competitive game.

3 Explain why the presence of others may impact positively and/or negatively on performance with regard to mental factors.

4 Evaluate the impact of decision making on performance.

1.2 Introduction to data collection

You need to know

- the reliability and practicality of the methods chosen to collect information
- the difference between qualitative and quantitative information
- the benefits and limitations of a model performer

Required protocols and organisational considerations

Throughout your Higher PE course you will have used a variety of methods to collect information on your performance. For example, you may have completed observation schedules, questionnaires or tests, or recorded some video.

Before you start to gather information on performance, you need to consider:

- the suitability of the methods chosen in relation to activity, factor and context
- the reliability and practicality of the methods chosen
- the qualitative and quantitative information the methods will provide you with.

The acronym 'RAVE' can help you remember what to consider when carrying out methods to collect information on your performance (Table 2).

Table 2 **Data collection considerations**

Reliability	■ Can the method be repeated again to allow for comparisons? ■ Was the data recorded?
Accuracy	■ Can you trust the person who is observing you to carry out their job effectively? ■ Do they have sufficient knowledge to carry out the method?
Validity	■ Is the method standardised? ■ Can it be completed under the exact same conditions?
Ease of use	■ Is it easy to set up? ■ Is it easy to understand the protocols? ■ Is it time consuming?

Quantitative and qualitative data

You must be able to demonstrate that you know the difference between quantitative and qualitative data, as described in Table 3. Both types will provide you with information when gathering data on your performance.

Table 3 Quantitative and qualitative data

Type of data	Description	Example
Quantitative	Data that can be specifically measured Facts and figures, such as percentages	It was identified from my general observation schedule that 75% of my smash shots in my badminton game were ineffective.
Qualitative	Data gathered from personal judgements, opinions and reflections	My coach told me that I was unable to hit the shuttle from above my head, which resulted in not having enough power to make an effective smash shot.

Quantitative data

■ Quantitative data are more reliable because an observer usually collects them in a more controlled way, and the evidence is clearly defined. For example, a general observation schedule or movement analysis sheet provides you with facts and figures.

■ When carrying out a match analysis, you should ensure that the data are more reliable by playing against equal opponents, playing full matches and playing several games, just in case you have an off day.

Objective performance measures include:
■ observation schedules
■ standardised fitness tests – for example, a sit and reach test to assess your hip flexibility
■ stopwatch
■ measuring tape

Qualitative data

■ Qualitative data are based on personal thoughts and opinions.
■ You can collect this type of data yourself or you may be given qualitative data from a peer, teacher or coach after you have performed.
■ The information you generate from qualitative data may not be consistent, because they are open to interpretation and will be dependent on the observer's personal opinion of how well you performed on the day.
■ Judges' personal opinions can affect how they score the quality and style of performance. For example, in dance and gymnastics a numerical judging score may be used, but this is not an objective measure.

Key terms

Observation schedule This compares your performance with criteria copied from a model performer. Development needs are easily identified.

Standardised fitness test A test with set rules/ protocols relating to the way it is performed. It must be carried out in the same way every time. For example, every time I carry out a bleep test I must ensure that the distance between the markers measures 20 m.

Stopwatch A time measuring device that helps provide factual data on how quick you are when completing a standardised test, such as the 30 m sprint test.

Measuring tape A distance measuring device that, for example, allows you to mark out 20 m accurately before completing a bleep test.

Model performer

Primarily, a model performance is used to make comparisons. You can look into similarities you share with a model performer and compare qualities that make you different.

Model performers can be used to:

- identify strengths and development needs
- increase confidence and motivation
- provide various types of feedback – qualitative and quantitative
- provide challenges in practice/competition
- continuously provide accurate feeds in practice
- inspire others to achieve their goals

Key terms

Model performer
Someone who can carry out a performance to the highest degree. They can demonstrate skill and experience relating to all four factors.

Qualities of a model performer

A model performer will possess many skills and attributes. They might be an elite athlete, such as Cristiano Ronaldo or Andy Murray, but could also be someone like a high-performing teammate, such as your captain.

Some of the qualities a model performer might possess are shown in Figure 4.

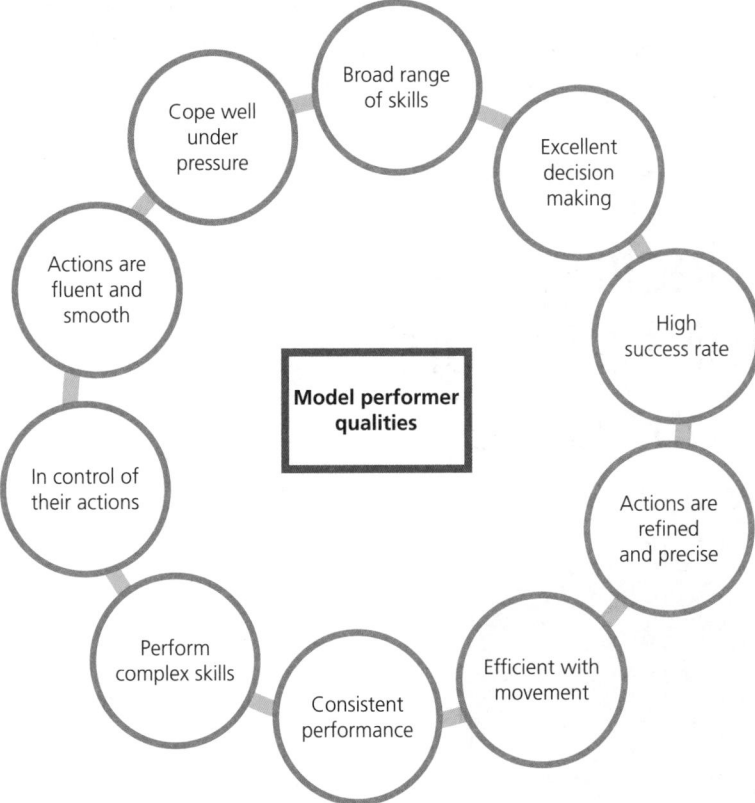

Figure 4 Qualities of a model performer

Table 4 shows the benefits and limitations to consider before using a model performer.

Table 4 Benefits and limitations of model performers

Model performers	
Benefits	**Limitations**
■ Model performers can be used as a *comparison tool*, comparing your performance with theirs using the model performer's criteria. ■ In this way they can be used as a *means to provide feedback*, allowing you to detect development needs and work on them. ■ They can be used as a *motivational aid*. Observing their performance can motivate you to work hard to achieve a high performance level. ■ They allow you to gauge whether any improvements are being made as you progress. ■ They allow you to realise how much work is required to achieve a model performance (benchmark).	■ It can be time consuming collecting and analysing information with regards to a model performer. ■ You might select a model performer who is not that good, and you could end up learning poor technique. ■ You might select an inappropriately high level of model performer, such as Lebron James, which can lead to setting unrealistic and unachievable goals. ■ You may not have sufficient knowledge to correctly analyse a model performer.

Do you know?

1 Describe the difference between *quantitative* and *qualitative* when gathering data on mental factors.

2 Explain the importance of gathering information on mental factors before you start a personal development plan.

3 Describe the qualities that a model performer possesses.

4 In relation to mental factors, compare your strengths and development needs with those of a model performer.

Exam tip

You need to be able to compare your own strengths and development needs in relation to those of a model performer.

1.3 Methods of collecting information to analyse factors impacting on performance

You need to know

■ what methods you have used to collect information on mental factors

■ how, when and where you carried out these methods

■ why you carried out these methods

■ what the benefits and limitations are of using these methods

Mental toughness questionnaire

A mental toughness questionnaire is used to gauge how effectively individuals deal with stress, pressure and challenge. The questionnaire describes the mindset that every person adopts in everything they do.

Description of method

- Download the mental toughness questionnaire from the internet. This can be found on the SATPE website.
- Respond to the list of 30 statements using *true* or *false*.
- When you have finished, check your answers in the evaluation section that follows.
- Statements will either have a score of 0 or 1.
- Add up your score to determine your strengths and development needs.

Some sample statements from the mental toughness questionnaire are listed in Table 5.

Table 5 **Sample statements from the mental toughness questionnaire**

Questions	True	False
1 I frequently worry about mistakes.		
2 I get really down on myself during performance when I mess up.		
3 It's easy for me to let go of my mistakes.		

> **Exam tip**
>
> When asked to describe a method to collect information on a factor, you should reference descriptions of how, when and where you completed it.

What does your score say about you?

- A score of 26–30 indicates strength in overall mental toughness.
- A score of 23–25 indicates average to moderate skill in mental toughness.
- A score of 22 or below indicates that there is a development need in the area of mental toughness. As a result, you should create a development plan to improve.

SCAT test

A SCAT test is used to measure the tendency of an athlete to experience anxiety when competing in sport.

Anxiety and arousal can have a big influence on performance levels. If anxiety and arousal are well balanced, performance can be at its peak. If the athlete is too anxious, bored or uninterested, performance can suffer. On the other hand, if they are over excited, their performance can also suffer.

Description of method

- Download the SCAT test from the internet. This can be found on the SATPE website.
- Respond to the list of 15 statements with *rarely*, *sometimes* or *often*.
- When you have finished, check your answers in the evaluation section that follows.
- Statements will have a score of 1, 2 or 3.
- Add up your score to determine your strengths and development needs.

Table 6 **Sample statements from the SCAT test**

Questions	Rarely	Sometimes	Often
1 Competing against other people/teams is socially enjoyable			
2 Before I compete, I feel uneasy			
3 Before I compete, I worry about not performing well			

What does your score say about you?

- A score of less than 17 indicates that you have low levels of anxiety.
- A score of 17–24 indicates that you have an average level of anxiety.
- A score of more than 24 indicates that you have a high level of anxiety. As a result, you should create a development plan to improve.

The benefits and limitations of the mental toughness questionnaire and SCAT test are listed in Table 7.

Table 7 **Benefits and limitations of mental factor data collection**

Mental factor data collection	
Benefits	**Limitations**
<ul><li>The written format provides a permanent record that allows for comparisons at a later date.</li><li>Strengths and development needs can be identified. A PDP and goals can be set thereafter.</li><li>Not time-consuming, so more time can be spent working on development needs.</li><li>Easy to follow, with limited instructions, so results gained will be reliable if answered honestly.</li></ul>	<ul><li>You might answer dishonestly, not giving a true reflection of your abilities and making the results invalid.</li><li>You may feel different going into each sporting context, depending on the severity of the pressure placed on you.</li><li>You may have a clouded view of how good you are. Do you score yourself better than you are or do you score yourself harshly?</li></ul>

1.4 Approaches used to develop performance

You need to know

■ how to describe and explain a variety of approaches used to develop performance with regard to mental factors

■ how to analyse and evaluate a variety of approaches used to develop performance with regard to mental factors

Developing performance in the mental factor is important. For example, carrying out mental approaches before a big performance can positively affect performance.

There are many different approaches used in this area. They often differ depending on the nature of the activity.

Mental rehearsal

Mental rehearsal is where the performer pictures themselves executing a skill and practises the skill in their mind, focusing on the specific stages and correct technique. To become proficient in the use of mental rehearsal you have to use it every day – on your way to training, during training and after training.

How to carry out mental rehearsal

- Select a quiet area, away from the competition/performance space.
- Establish a clear picture in your mind of a quality performance.
- Break the performance into manageable parts.
- Be positive, imagining yourself doing well.
- Relax, for example by listening to music. Releasing body tension allows you to feel at ease and distracts the mind from the activity/competition.
- Concentrate on slow and deep breathing to relax and focus the mind, allowing you to be composed and ready for performance.

When to carry out mental rehearsal

- In every training session, before you execute any skill or combination of skills. See, feel, and experience yourself moving through the actions in your mind, as you would like them actually to unfold.
- In the competition situation – use imagery before the start of the event and see yourself performing successfully/winning.

The benefits and limitations of mental rehearsal are listed in Table 8.

Table 8 The benefits and limitations of mental rehearsal

Mental rehearsal	
Benefits	Limitations
■ The approach is versatile and can be carried out anywhere – not only in the training room or during a game, but also at home because no specialist equipment is required. ■ It gives you an opportunity to confront a situation in your head and deal with it appropriately before it happens in real life.	■ Performers need to find an area that is free from distractions. This can be difficult in a training or competition environment. ■ Performers may not give the approach sufficient time to practise it, resulting in limited development. ■ Performers may find it difficult to create a positive image of the situation in their head, which can lead to frustration.

Positive self-talk

- Positive self-talk relates to the ability to overcome negative thinking.
- When negative events or mistakes happen in training or performance, positive self-talk seeks to bring the positive out of the negative, to help you do better next time, to go further, or just to keep moving forward.
- Positive self-talk will affirm that you possess the skills, abilities, positive attitudes and beliefs that are the building blocks of success.
- The statements you choose need to be vivid and be practised well in advance of the competition.
- Most of all, they must be totally believable. You should use these especially in low-confidence situations.

How to carry out positive self-talk

The key is to take a negative mindset and change it into a positive mindset by using key phrases, such as those shown in Table 9.

Table 9 **Converting a negative mindset into a positive one**

Negative mindset	Positive mindset
'I can't tackle him'	'I can tackle him – I will drive low to high to secure the ball'
'I can't win this race'	'I will set out strong and commit'
'I'm scared to perform in front of an audience'	'I'm confident I can show the audience how well I can do my routine'

When to carry out positive self-talk

Use positive self-talk:
- during both training and competition
- when you start to feel that something is going wrong in your performance
- when you feel yourself slipping into a state of discomfort.

> ### Exam tip
>
> Make your own list of four or five positive self-statements and read them to yourself every night before you go to bed and every morning as you wake up. Through repeated use, they will become embedded in your subconscious and have a profound influence on your sporting performance.

The benefits and limitations of positive self-talk are listed in Table 10.

Table 10 The benefits and limitations of positive self-talk

Positive self-talk	
Benefits	**Limitations**
■ The approach is versatile and can be done anywhere – not only in the training room or game, but also at home because no specialist equipment is required. ■ It gives you an opportunity to confront a situation in your head and deal with it appropriately before it happens in real life.	■ Performers may not give the approach sufficient time to practise it, resulting in limited development. ■ Unless a performer is willing to challenge the thought process they go through when they make a mistake, then little to no progress will be made. ■ Performers may find it embarrassing to say positive phrases about themselves, which can lead to little progression.

Do you know?

1 Identify *two* approaches you have used to develop performance in relation to mental factors.

2 Describe *one* approach you have used to develop performance in relation to mental factors.

3 Choose a mental approach. Explain why you would use this to develop performance.

4 What are the benefits and limitations of *one* approach to developing performance in relation to mental factors?

End of section 1 questions

1 a Describe *one* method used to gather information about the impact of mental factors on performance.

 b Describe the information you gathered using the method described in part (a).

2 Evaluate your strengths and development needs in comparison with a model performer in terms of mental factors.

3 Describe the impact of mental factors on your own performance.

4 Analyse mental approaches that can be used to overcome the negative impact of the presence of others during performance.

2 Emotional factors

2.1 Factors impacting on performance

You need to know
- definitions of emotional factors (examples are given for resilience, confidence, aggression, fear)
- how emotional factors can impact positively or negatively on performance
- the impact of emotional factors on other factors

Resilience

- **Resilience** enables a performer to bounce back from, say, a defeat, injury or poor performance.
- A good example is Rafael Nadal. Nadal has struggled with back, wrist and knee injuries throughout his tennis career. Between 2014 and 2016 he missed 14 months of elite-level tennis. Despite being labelled as facing a 'career-ending injury' by players and journalists, Nadal returned in 2017. He went on to reclaim his world number 1 ranking and won both the French and US Opens in 2017. His ability to battle back from such adversity highlights his amazing emotional strength.

You can use the FACI structure to think about resilience and its impact on performance. Here is an example:

F	Emotional (resilience)
A	Table tennis
C	I lost my first game 11–1. I was so frustrated with how I played, I kept pushing my backhand drive into the net. This is normally my strongest shot.
I	I continued to praise myself, despite my disappointment. I kept playing with aggression and I knew I would find my rhythm and consistency. My performance did indeed improve, and I hit winner after winner off my backhand side. I won the next three games 11–9, 11–6, 11–4.

Figure 5 highlights the importance of resilience in an elite performance context.

> ### Key term
> **Resilience** The ability to never give up despite hard times, and to maintain a positive outlook throughout.

> ### Exam tip
> FACI stands for Factor, Activity, Context, Impact. FACI can be applied to any factors you cover in this section.

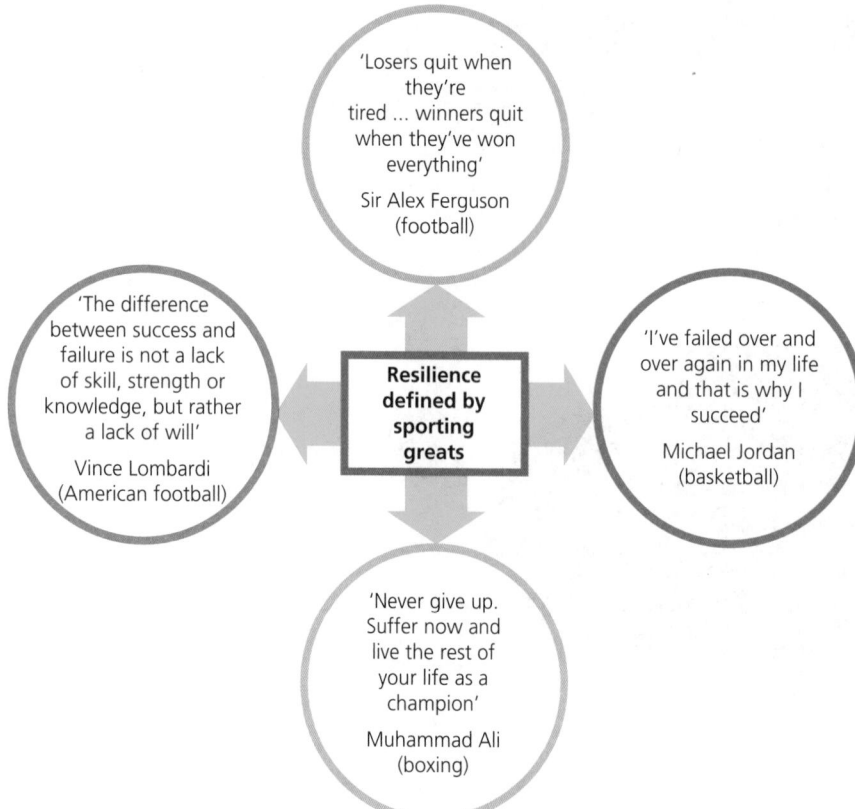

Figure 5 Definitions of resilience

Confidence

- **Confidence** is having belief in your own ability and being willing to face challenges.
- Having high confidence levels will generally have a positive impact on performance.
- Performers must be confident to successfully compete against different opposition in different situations and conditions. However, being overly confident can sometimes lead to performers underestimating their opposition, resulting in a performance or movement that lacks the required intensity or concentration. This often results in a negative outcome.

> ### Key term
>
> **Confidence** Self-belief, which allows individuals to face challenging situations and back themselves throughout.

You can use the FACI structure to think about confidence and its impact on performance. Here are two examples:

F	Emotional (confidence)
A	Dance
C	While performing at a ballet competition, I did not feel confident performing in front of such a large audience.
I	Because I was conscious of my appearance, I was not fully focused on my routine and did not showcase my ability level. My movements appeared rushed and unbalanced and I did not get the score I had hoped for.

F	Emotional (confidence)
A	Basketball
C	As a guard it is my responsibility to carry the ball up the court and call plays to unlock the opposition defence. I need to be confident in my own ability to create scoring opportunities. Guards need to have a full skill repertoire (dribble, shoot and pass).
I	Having confidence as a guard allowed me to hold on to the ball late in the match. I knew I would make my jump shot and so I let the clock run down before finding space and releasing the ball. Scoring with only seconds to go meant that our opposition did not have time to launch an attack, and we won the match.

Aggression

- **Aggression** refers to hostile or violent behaviour caused by feelings of anger or frustration.
- Competition rules vary depending on the sport and the level of performance.
- Look at Figure 6. Consider potential sanctions for the aggressive, hostile or violent behaviour in these performance contexts.
- Consider your own sport and performance level and think about sanctions you may face if you are overly aggressive, hostile or violent. How might these sanctions impact on performance?

Key term

Aggression Behaviour resulting from feelings of anger or frustration.

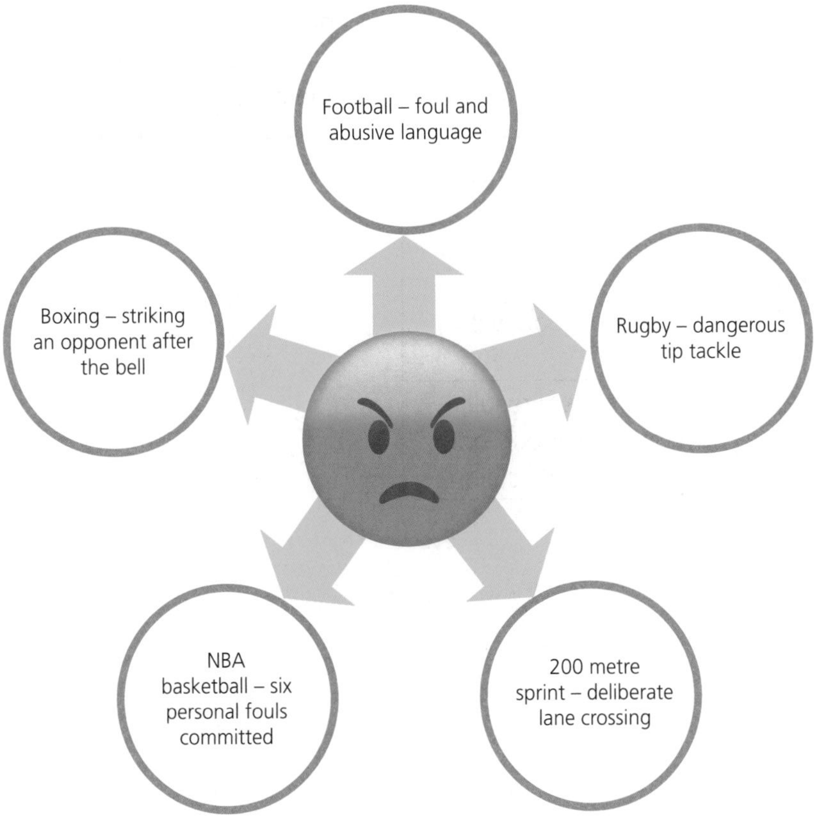

Figure 6 **Examples of aggressive behaviour**

You can use the FACI structure to think about aggression and its impact on performance. Here is an example:

F	Emotional (aggression)
A	Tennis
C	I was playing poorly and became more and more frustrated. Eventually I got so annoyed that I smashed my tennis racket on the floor, breaking the frame.
I	The umpire awarded the game to my opponent despite our game being tied at 30–30. This meant that my opponent won the first set 6–4. I was warned by the umpire that any further outbursts would result in a disqualification.

Fear

- Most performers will experience **fear** at some point. It is most common when expectations are high, for example performing in front of a large crowd, a cup final or return after an injury lay-off.
- Fear can impact negatively on a performer's preparation. Feelings of worry can lead to **somatic anxiety**, stress and distraction. This often results in a timid or error-filled performance, because emotions are not balanced.
- Fear affects our emotional wellbeing, but it also has huge impact on mental, social and physical performance too.

You can use the FACI structure to think about fear and its impact on performance. Here are two examples:

F	Emotional (fear)
A	Trampolining
C	I am constantly concerned about over-rotating during my front somersault. This can have safety implications because if a performer doesn't fully commit to the skill, the likelihood is they will under-rotate.
I	I was scared, bouncing into my front somersault. As a result, I was not as tucked as I should have been and lost speed and rhythm during my rotation, dropping vital marks for execution.

Key terms

Fear An unpleasant emotion caused by the threat of failure, danger or injury.

Somatic anxiety A physiological/emotional response to a threat or fear. Common responses include increased heart rate, 'butterflies in the stomach' and dry mouth.

F	Emotional (fear)
A	Boxing
C	Fear of getting hurt or injured is common in boxing, as is the fear of losing an unbeaten run or a flawless win record. Many boxers use the pressure of failure in a positive context. I am proud of my unbeaten run and train hard to remain undefeated.
I	Fear of defeat or injury keeps me focused when in the ring. If I know that my opponent can hurt me my movement remains sharp and I maintain concentration and focus throughout the fight. Because I respect all of my opponents' power and speed, I am able to use my jab to maintain distance and launch counterattacks with composure. This allows me to build a big points lead and win the fight.

Figure 7 highlights the potential impact of emotional factors on mental, social and physical factors.

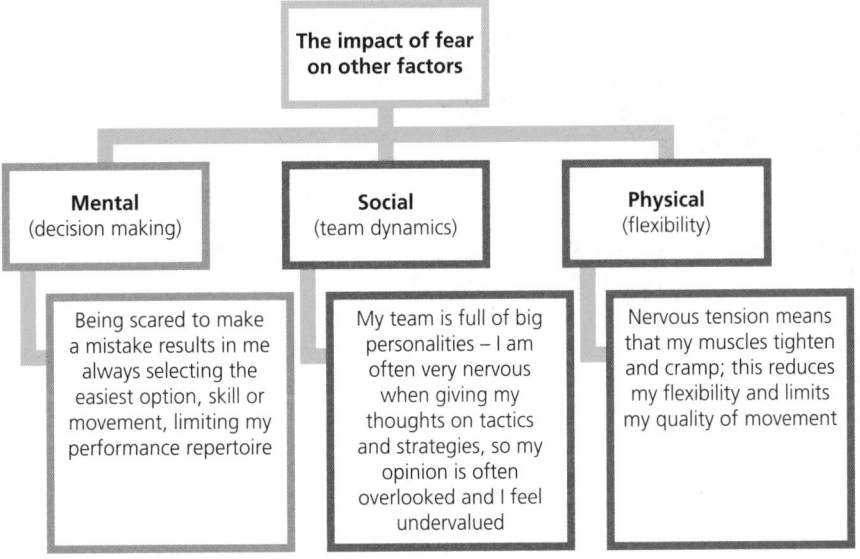

Figure 7 Impact of fear on mental, social and physical factors

Do you know?

1 Describe *one* strength and *one* area of development in relation to emotional factors.
2 Explain how emotional factors can impact on performance.
3 Analyse the impact emotional factors can have on each of the other three factors during a performance.
4 Evaluate the impact of fear and aggression on performance.

Exam tip

If asked to *analyse* the impact of a factor on performance, you must look beyond an explanation. Think about identification, implication and impact:
- **Identification** – a noisy crowd can impact a performer negatively.
- **Implication** – if the performer is worried about negative crowd reaction they may produce an underwhelming performance.
- **Impact** – the performer will not be able to contribute effectively. They may refuse opportunities to shoot and opt for easy passes to teammates. The fear of failure prevents them from excelling.

2.2 Methods of collecting information to analyse factors impacting on performance

You need to know

■ different methods of collecting information to analyse factors impacting on performance
■ how, when, where and why you carried out these methods
■ what the benefits and limitations are to using certain methods
■ how to use information gathered to plan for a personal development plan

Exam tip

When collecting data you should look to compare your performance against a model performer. A model performer could be a classmate, teammate, teacher, coach or elite performer.

■ Model performers exemplify quality performance. In an emotional context they will have the ability to deal with setbacks and have huge self-belief even when challenged with adversity.
■ They use fear as a positive, and display controlled aggression to outperform opponents.
■ For example, Andy Murray suffered a devastating defeat to Roger Federer in the 2012 Wimbledon final. However, he promised to return stronger the next year and set clear goals to improve his serving. The following year, he returned and produced a stunning performance to beat Novak Djokovic in straight sets to become the first British male champion for 77 years.

Sports emotion questionnaire

■ A sports emotion questionnaire can be completed directly before or directly after a performance and aims to identify which specific emotional factors may be impacting on the performer's behaviour and therefore overall performance, for example resilience, confidence, aggression or fear.

- Performers are asked to circle how they are feeling (22 emotions in total) on a scale of 0 (never) to 4 (always).
- The questionnaire is very easy to understand and therefore only takes a few minutes to complete.
- It is completed on paper and can be kept safe for future comparisons to monitor emotional development.

Table 11 shows an extract from a sports emotion questionnaire.

Table 11 Extract from a sports emotion questionnaire

Emotion	Never	Sometimes	Often	Very often	Always
Uneasy	0	1	2	3	4
Tense	0	1	2	3	4
Nervous	0	1	2	3	4
Apprehensive	0	1	2	3	4
Irritated	0	1	2	3	4
Furious	0	1	2	3	4
Annoyed	0	1	2	3	4
Angry	0	1	2	3	4
Anxious	0	1	2	3	4

Scoring examples

$$anxiety = \frac{uneasy + tense + nervous + apprehensive + anxious}{5}$$

$$anger = \frac{irritated + furious + annoyed + angry}{4}$$

Anxiety example

uneasy (4) + tense (4) + nervous (4) + apprehensive (4) + anxious (4) = 20

$$\frac{20}{5} = 4$$

Assessment: with an average score of 4, this athlete has extreme levels of performance anxiety.

Anger example

irritated (2) + furious (2) + annoyed (4) + angry (4) = 12

$$\frac{12}{4} = 3$$

Assessment: with an average score of 3, this athlete has significant levels of performance anger.

The benefits and limitations of the sports emotion questionnaire are listed in Table 12.

Table 12 The benefits and limitations of the sports emotion questionnaire

Sports emotion questionnaire	
Benefits	**Limitations**
■ It is quick and easy to fill in, either directly before or after performance. ■ It provides benchmark data that can be saved and compared to check for improvements. ■ It provides a clear emotional focus to tailor approaches.	■ The performer must be honest regarding their emotional state. ■ Performers may experience personal challenges that impact on their emotional state. This could be completely separate from the pressures of performance, for example a family bereavement or a relationship breakup.

> **Key term**
>
> **Benchmark data** Data providing initial information on performance. This information can be stored for comparison at a later date.

Disciplinary record

- A disciplinary record is collated over a series of performances/ matches.
- The aim is to spot patterns in emotional performance and then select and implement suitable approaches to develop and improve behaviour management.
- If a pattern is spotted, the player, coach or teacher can intervene, and improvements can be made. Late cautions and sending offs are often related to physical fitness – a lack of cardio respiratory endurance, which then impacts on emotional control.
- The disciplinary record covers many emotion-related behaviours, such as serious foul play, violent conduct, abusive language, unsporting behaviour, and lack of engagement with teammates.

The benefits and limitations of disciplinary records are listed in Table 13.

Table 13 The benefits and limitations of disciplinary records

Disciplinary records	
Benefits	**Limitations**
■ A disciplinary record encourages reflection and accountability. Performers have to consider genuinely how their emotions impact on their performance and the performance of others, such as teammates, opponents and officials. ■ A record provides coaches, managers and performers with qualitative and quantitative information, allowing them to identify areas of development, such as anger management. ■ The coach/manager can track the emotional performances of individual performers. Approaches can then be designed to prepare performers for stressful situations, such as a cup final, a league decider or an intimidating home crowd.	■ The official must referee/score fairly and consistently in line with the laws of the game/sport for accurate emotional data to be collected. ■ Performers can become demotivated if they believe they are being harshly treated by officials, management, teammates etc. ■ The quality of a disciplinary record relies on accurate data collection by the match official or observer. They must be knowledgeable and concentrating.

Do you know?

1 Identify *two* ways of gathering information relating to emotional factors.
2 Select *one* way of gathering information on emotional factors. Describe how you have gathered data using this method.
3 Explain the challenges you may face when gathering data on emotional factors.
4 Evaluate the effectiveness of *two* emotional factor data collection methods.

Exam tip

When describing methods for gathering information, you need to provide statements on what the method looks like, where you accessed the method and how you carried it out.

2.3 Approaches used to develop performance

You need to know

- how to identify and carry out approaches that are appropriate for developing performance with regard to emotional factors
- how to describe a variety of approaches for developing performance with regard to emotional factors
- how to explain the use of certain approaches
- how to analyse and evaluate approaches used to develop performance with regard to mental factors
- how to adapt or modify approaches used to improve performance

Exam tip

Consider how emotions affect your wellbeing on a daily basis. Your emotional state (resilience levels, confidence levels, aggression levels, happiness levels etc.) at the beginning of a day often has a direct impact on your performance. The same can be said in a sporting context. If we are to improve performance, we must consider our emotional state and implement approaches that can genuinely improve our overall output.

Remember, that for approaches to improve performance they must be:
- specific – to your factor focus
- realistic – in a training or performance context
- adaptable – can be simplified or overloaded to suit performance levels
- recordable – diary entries, reflections, retesting etc. can measure the effect of an approach on performance

Team talks

Description of approach:

- In a team sport context, an effective team talk is usually given by the coach, manager or captain.
- The team talk will focus on team ethos, often underpinned by work rate and technical ability.
- Team talks are typically given prior to a performance and at half-time or during a time out period.
- Tactics will be discussed in detail and will often differ depending on the quality of opposition, weather, playing surface, playing numbers, scoreline, time of play etc.
- Performers will be reminded of their individual responsibilities within a predetermined formation, structure or tactic.
- Some performers may be challenged to improve their performance levels based on prior competitions/fixtures. Others may be commended for their consistency and encouraged to improve further.
- The overall aim is to ensure that every individual feels emotionally ready to perform to their best.
- Generally, performers who are confident and happy, and feel valued by their coach, manager or captain will produce a better performance.

The benefits and limitations of team talks are listed in Table 14.

Table 14 **The benefits and limitations of team talks**

Team talks	
Benefits	**Limitations**
<ul><li>Afford coaches and managers the opportunity to refocus performers before or mid-way through a performance.</li><li>Allow performers to paint a mental picture of their performance, calming their nerves and building reassurance.</li><li>Increase self-confidence and build resilience against challenging opposition.</li><li>Build individual accountability in terms of roles and responsibilities.</li></ul>	<ul><li>Lofty coach/manager expectations can build fear and anxiety in individuals.</li><li>A large focus on the opposition can create an inferiority complex and a lack of confidence.</li><li>An overly aggressive team talk could potentially lead to poor individual decision making and dangerous play.</li><li>Increased individual accountability may result in fear of being dropped or substituted.</li></ul>

Centering

- Centering is an emotional coping strategy/approach used to manage feelings of fear.
- Performers have to continually cope with the pressures of failure, defeat, injury, disqualification, substitution and rejection.

- Centering is often undertaken pre-performance and is used to calm emotions and bring clarity to thinking patterns.
- Centering is a five-stage process that aims to replace feelings of fear and apprehension with feelings of confidence and resilience.
- The performer must consciously learn to relax their body and working muscles.

Description of approach:

1 Focus on a chosen point. This could be an item – an object or structure – but should not be a person (teammate, opponent, official, manager, family member, observer, spectator etc.).

2 Close your eyes and visualise a detailed positive outcome, such as winning, making a big tackle, scoring a goal, producing a refined sequence or lifting the trophy. This image should 'play on repeat'.

3 Breathe slowly and deliberately. Consciously think about inhaling through the nose and exhaling through the mouth. Slow and relax your breathing, with eyes remaining closed.

4 As you slowly and deliberately control your breathing, focus on individual muscle groups and relax and release all tension and anxiety. Start from your calves and finish at your neck. Eyes remain closed.

5 Remain focused on your positive outcome. Previous performances should be discounted. Maintain focus on the present and be assertive from the moment your performance begins, for example ensuring a good first touch, pressurising opposition players early or landing your first rotational skill.

The benefits and limitations of centering are listed in Table 15.

Table 15 The benefits and limitations of centering

Centering	
Benefits	**Limitations**
■ Easy to set up and so can be done in the build-up to a performance. ■ Very versatile – can be used to focus on a particular skill, behaviour or tactic – facilitating a quality performance. ■ Relaxes muscle groups, resulting in a more fluid performance. Reduced anxiety leads to reduced muscular tension. ■ Centering allows you to deal effectively with a problem or an event in your head before you confront it in real life. It allows you to paint a picture of how you will deal effectively with the challenge.	■ A quiet space is required to ensure emotional focus. This can be difficult with team talks, changing room music, teammates chatting, crowd noise etc. ■ Centering must be practised and perfected. Emotional preparation can be overlooked and so an athlete may not give sufficient time to this emotional approach to feel the relaxation benefits. ■ Performers can find it difficult to create positive images of their performance. This can lead to frustration and may be detrimental to performance. Negative thoughts of past defeats or injuries can creep in if the performer is nervous or emotionally unstable.

Do you know?

1 Identify *two* approaches you have used to develop emotional factors.

2 Describe how emotional factors might affect your ability to carry out your performance development plan with quality.

3 Describe *two* approaches you have used to develop your performance in relation to emotional factors.

4 Explain why a performer may need to adapt or modify certain approaches during a performance development plan.

End of section 2 questions

1 Describe *two* strengths or *two* areas of development in relation to emotional factors.

2 Select *one* way of gathering information on emotional factors. Describe how you have gathered data using this method.

3 From the data you have gathered, explain your strengths and development needs in relation to emotional factors.

4 Evaluate the differences between your emotional control and the emotional control of a model performer within a challenging performance context.

5 Focusing on *one* specific approach, evaluate its effectiveness in developing your emotional performance.

3 Social factors

3.1 Factors impacting on performance

You need to know

- definitions of social factors (examples are given for team dynamics, roles and responsibilities, communication)
- how each social factor might affect performance negatively
- how each social factor might affect performance positively

Team dynamics

- **Team dynamics** affect team cohesion.
- This is where players are drawn to a common goal.
- Coaches often talk about teams needing time to 'gel' in order to perform at their maximum potential.
- It has often been demonstrated that skill and ability will only get you so far; groups of players must have an intangible bond. This develops naturally as a result of coaching and day-to-day interactions.

Figure 8 highlights the qualities that a team must have in order to demonstrate effective team dynamics.

> ### Key term
>
> **Team dynamics** The social interactions created by personalities, relationships and roles. These affect the ability of the whole team to work cohesively towards a common goal.

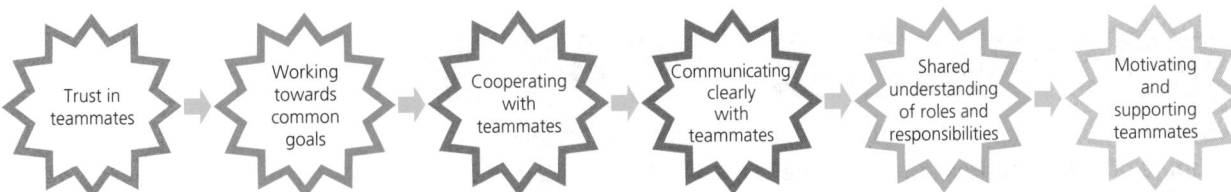

Figure 8 Qualities required for effective team dynamics

Figure 9 highlights the key qualities to consider when creating a team who should work together towards achieving a common goal.

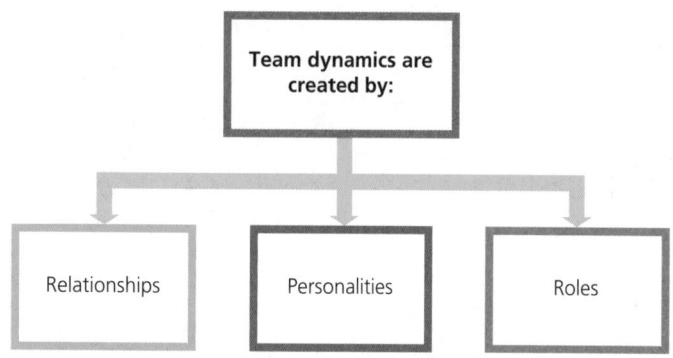

Figure 9 Aspects of team dynamics

You can use the FACI structure to think about team dynamics.
Here are two examples:

F	Social (team dynamics)
A	Cheerleading
C	It is important to have good team dynamics when performing a cheer routine. As a flyer I need to have trust and belief in my teammates that they will support and catch me while performing my stunt in the air.
I	Having good trust in my teammates ensures that I am confident in performing this complex skill. I can perform the complex stunt, which will look aesthetically pleasing and score me high points in the competition because the stunt was executed safely with control.

F	Social (team dynamics)
A	Basketball
C	I do not gel well with one person in my basketball team. This makes it difficult to work together as one unit when we play. I do not pass him the ball even when he is in space.
I	A lack of team dynamics has often cost me and my team possession of the ball or a chance at scoring a basket.

Exam tip

When asked to explain the impact of a factor on performance, you should provide a context that sets the scene and then explain the impact of that context on performance. This can be either positive or negative.

Roles and responsibilities

■ The individual role you adopt in a group or team activity will be dependent on many factors. These may include your physical attributes and your ability as a skilled performer, including your decision-making qualities.

■ When each individual's attributes and qualities are considered, then a relevant structure or strategy can be planned. For example, in basketball every player has a **role and responsibility** (Table 16). If each player carries out their role and responsibility effectively, this will lead to a successful outcome.

> **Key term**
>
> **Role and responsibility** A performer's function when playing as part of a group or team. It is essential to understand what your role is and how it relates to the roles of your teammates.

Table 16 Roles and responsibilities in basketball

Activity	Role	Responsibility example
Basketball	Guard	To dribble the ball up the court in an attack
	Forward	To shoot and score as many baskets as possible
	Centre	To collect the offensive and defensive rebounds

You can use the FACI structure to think about roles and responsibilities. Here are two examples:

F	Social (roles and responsibilities)
A	Netball
C	In netball every player has a specific role and responsibility based on where they are allowed to go on the court. If a player is offside then that would be a foul and the ball would be turned over to the other team. For example, when playing as a WA I am not allowed into the shooting circle.
I	If I enter the shooting circle during play then that would be a foul. This means that my team will lose possession and an opportunity to score a goal.

F	Social (roles and responsibilities)
A	Football
C	As a midfielder, it is my responsibility to track back and support the defence when we lose possession of the ball.
I	Because I have tracked back in defence, this makes it harder for the opposition to break through the defensive line, as there are no gaps, making it harder for them to score.

Communication

- Communication is the ability to convey information to teammates/ the coach through speech, signals or action during practice and performance.
- It is vital to share meaningful information with your teammates. Communication allows you to finalise roles, discuss tactics or refine technique. For example, a point guard in basketball will communicate throughout the match using a combination of hand signals and verbal cues to call plays in an attacking strategy.

Communicating with your team is often to your benefit. Building up team spirit and a solid bond between your teammates can help you achieve success in big competitions. Communication can be verbal or non verbal (Figure 10).

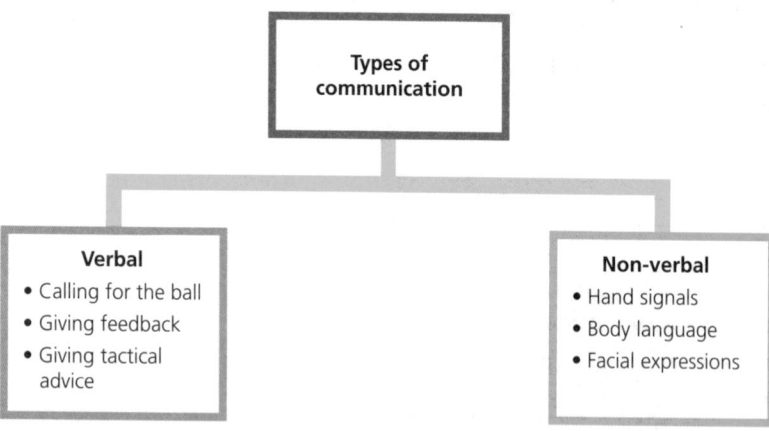

Figure 10 Types of communication

Exam tip

Use the acronym BUGS to help you structure your answer to an exam question:

B   Box the command word and factor.

U   Underline the key words in the question.

G   Glance at the number of marks.

S   Sentence Starter to introduce your answer.

Figure 11 shows how communication can be used in a performance context.

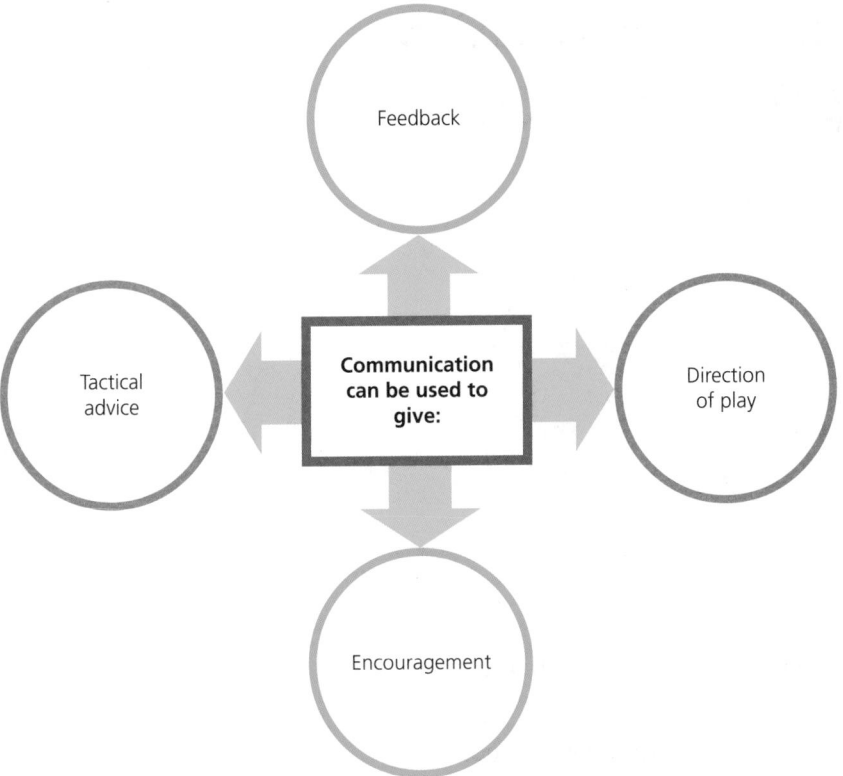

Figure 11 Communication in a performance context

You can use the FACI structure to think about communication. Here are two examples:

F	Social (communication)
A	Basketball
C	I need to have good communication to be able to call for the ball when I am in an open space. As a forward, I need to communicate with the guard during a fast break to let her know that I am ready to receive the ball to drive towards the basket for an unopposed lay-up.
I	Because I did not communicate with the guard to let her know I was in space, the guard passed the ball to the other forward who was being pressured by the opposition and, as a result, the ball was intercepted and an attack was started by the other team.

F	Social (communication)
A	Volleyball
C	I need to be able to communicate clearly in volleyball by calling for the ball to let my teammates know that I am in the best position to receive it.
I	If I do not call for the ball early, then there could be confusion, resulting in nobody going for the ball and our team losing a valuable point.

Do you know?

1 Define *two* different social factors.

2 Describe how team dynamics might impact positively and/or negatively on performance.

3 Explain how roles and responsibilities can impact negatively on a performance.

4 Explain how communication can impact positively on a performance.

3.2 Methods of collecting information to analyse factors impacting on performance

You need to know
- what methods you have used to collect information on social factors
- how, when and where you carried out these methods
- why you carried out these methods
- what the benefits and limitations are of using these methods

Team/group feedback

- Team/group feedback provides you with valuable information about how well you work within a group.
- Download the team/group feedback method from the internet. This can be found on the SATPE website.
- Answer the list of nine questions with a descriptive comment.
- The nine questions include the following:
  - During my performance how did I cope when working as part of a group?
  - Did I communicate?
  - Did I accept others' opinions?
- When you have finished, use this to make a plan to improve your development needs.

The benefits and limitations of team/group feedback are listed in Table 17.

Table 17 **The benefits and limitations of team/group feedback**

Team/group feedback	
Benefits	Limitations
<ul><li>It can focus on a variety of social factors.</li><li>Valuable information can be gained on how well you work in a team.</li><li>It can provide you with strengths and development needs in relation to social factors.</li><li>You can keep the results as a permanent record and compare with future retests to check for improvements.</li></ul>	<ul><li>Performers may feel anxious at receiving feedback in front of the group, particularly if it relates to what needs to be improved.</li><li>Constructive feedback may not be well received if relationships with the person completing it are not strong. This could impact team dynamics.</li></ul>

Exam tip

When answering an explain question, use linking terms such as 'because' and 'this allows'. These will mean that you can put your explanatory point across well.

Social questionnaire

Description of the method:

- The social questionnaire provides you with valuable information on how well you work in a team.
- Download the questionnaire from the internet. This can be found on the SATPE website.
- Answer the list of 15 statements with either: Rarely, Sometimes, Often or Always.
- The statements include:
  - ☐ We all share the same commitment to our team's goals.
  - ☐ This team gives me enough opportunities to improve my own performance.
  - ☐ I am happy with my teammates' level of desire to win.
- When you have finished, check your answers in the evaluation section that follows
- Statements will have a scoring system of 1–4.
- Add up your scores to determine your strengths and development needs.

The benefits and limitations of the social questionnaire are listed in Table 18.

Table 18 **The benefits and limitations of the social questionnaire**

Social questionnaire	
Benefits	**Limitations**
<ul><li>It can focus on a variety of social factors.</li><li>Valuable information can be gained on how well you work in a team.</li><li>It can provide you with strengths and development needs in relation to social factors.</li><li>You can keep it as a permanent record and compare with future retests to check for improvements.</li></ul>	<ul><li>Performers may lack the experience or expertise required to carry out the method.</li><li>Performers may not answer truthfully in order to make themselves look better, at the expense of gathering reliable results.</li><li>This method relies on the subjective opinion of the performer.</li></ul>

Do you know?

1 Describe *two* different methods you have used to gather information on social factors.

2 Explain the appropriateness of *one* method used to gather information on social factors.

3 What are the benefits and limitations of *one* method used to gather information on social factors?

4 What strengths and development needs did you identify from your data collection?

3.3 Approaches used to develop performance

Building team dynamics

■ Building team dynamics refers to various activities undertaken to motivate team members and increase overall performance of the team.

■ A motivating factor is a must. Team-building activities consist of various tasks undertaken to groom team members and motivate them to perform to the best of their ability.

■ Team leaders need to undertake fun team-building activities that help their team gel.

■ Alternatively, team building can be integrated into daily tasks. Various activities can be undertaken to address different team issues, while ensuring an element of fun to increase the effectiveness of the activity.

Tangled knot

1 Divide the team into groups of four to nine players.
2 Each group forms a circle facing each other.
3 Players reach across and grab another player's hand or forearm.
4 Once each player is holding on to another player, each player reaches across the circle again and grabs a different player's hand or forearm, so that each player is holding on to two different players.
5 At this point the groups should look as if they are tangled in a knot.
6 Through talking and teamwork, the group tries to untangle itself without breaking any of the handholds.
7 When the exercise is complete the group is in a circle again.

Hula hoop exercise

1 Divide the team into groups of six.
2 Lay seven hoops out on the ground in a line (see Figure 12).
3 All six players should stand in one hoop each, leaving the centre hoop free.
4 The group must come to a solution for getting all group members to their mirror hoop on the opposite side by sticking to the following conditions:
   ☐ You cannot have more than one person in a hoop at one time.
   ☐ You cannot step outside of the hoops to move.
   ☐ You cannot stand in the centre hoop for more than 1 second.
   ☐ You cannot jump a hoop to move space.

Figure 12 Hula hoop exercise

The benefits and limitations of building team dynamics are listed in Table 19.

Table 19 The benefits and limitations of building team dynamics

Building team dynamics	
Benefits	**Limitations**
■ Team-building exercises are easy to set up and complete, and do not require a lot of equipment. This means they are an efficient use of time, and results and improvements can be seen quickly. ■ This approach allows the team to work together and get to know each other without the pressure of playing in a competitive game. ■ It allows players to understand their teammates' personalities, and how these can be best applied when going into a competitive situation. ■ Everyone in the team is involved, so they feel included; this will boost confidence.	■ This will only have a positive impact if all players commit to the exercise. ■ Some teammates may feel that these exercises waste valuable time that could be better spent training for a competitive game; thus they can become disengaged. ■ There is no pressure, so this approach does not reflect a game situation. ■ It is difficult to get any objective data (statistics) to see if improvements are taking place when using this approach.

Communication

Team talks

- Team talks are vital in ensuring that your team is well organised before going into a game.
- This is a great opportunity for your coach/captain to inform all teammates of the expectations for the game.
- They may communicate the direction of play, strategies and tactics. This will go a long way to ensure that the team works as one cohesive unit.

Communication drills

Description of drill 1

Working in a small group, players move around the area and pass the ball to other members of the group, in a particular sequence. For example:

- 1 passes to 2
- 2 passes to 3
- 3 passes to 4
- 4 passes to 1

The condition is that players must *call for the ball before the player makes a pass.*

Description of drill 2

Same as drill 1, but this time players can now pass the ball to anyone in their group.

The condition is that players must *call the name of the person before making the pass.*

Description of drill 3

Same as drill 2, i.e. players can pass the ball to anyone in their group.

The condition is that players must *use a non-verbal signal to receive a pass.*

When communicating with people in your team, it is important you take into consideration the three Cs (Figure 13):

- Communication needs to be clear and concise so that the teammates understand the information you are trying to convey.
- Communication needs to be constructive when you share feedback/information. This will help performers feel that you are trying to help them improve.

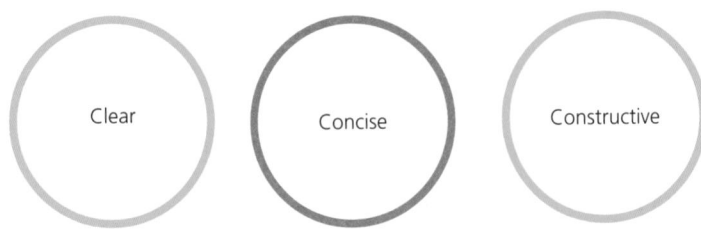

Figure 13 The three Cs

Do you know?

1 Describe *one* approach you have used to develop performance with regard to social factors.

2 Explain *one* approach you have used to develop performance with regard to social factors.

3 Analyse *one* approach to developing performance with regard to social factors.

4 Evaluate a different approach to developing performance with regard to social factors.

End of section 3 questions

1 Explain why it is important to gather information about the impact of social factors on performance before starting a personal development plan.

2 Describe two different methods used to gather information on social factors.

3 Describe the positive and/or negative impact of social factors on performance.

4 Explain the impact that social factors could have on performance when carrying out a development plan.

5 Describe two approaches which could be used to develop social factors.

4 Physical factors: skills

4.1 Factors impacting on performance

You need to know

- definitions of physical skills factors (quality of performance, technical qualities and special qualities)
- how each physical skills factor might affect performance negatively
- how each physical skills factor might affect performance positively

Quality of performance

- Quality of performance takes into consideration fluency, effort, accuracy and control.
- Having fluency when performing allows you to sustain an effective performance for a long period of time.
- If you are able to play with accuracy and control, this will lead to successful outcomes.
- With regards to effort, if you can move around using maximum efficiency and minimum effort then you will preserve your energy and be able to use it for skill execution.

You can use the FACI structure to think about quality of performance. Here are two examples:

F	Physical (quality of performance)
A	Badminton
C	It is important that I have good accuracy in my shot placement in badminton so that I can strike the shuttle as far away from my opponent as possible. For example, if I can play a drop shot close to the net while my opponent is at the back of the court, then this will limit the amount of time they have to respond.
I	If my opponent does not have time to get to the front of the court to return the shuttle then I will win the rally, gaining a point.

Key terms

Fluency The quality of being able to link one skill smoothly with another.

Effort The determination demonstrated in an attempt to be successful.

Accuracy Precision when executing a skill or technique.

Control The quality of being able to execute a skill in a controlled manner.

Exam tip

FACI stands for Factor, Activity, Context, Impact. FACI can be applied to any factors you cover in this section.

F	Physical (quality of performance)
A	Gymnastics
C	It is important that I have good control when performing a handstand into forward roll in gymnastics. I need to be able to hold the handstand position with control before linking it into the forward roll.
I	If I am unable to perform the handstand with control then it will have a knock-on effect on the rest of the skill. The skill will look messy and I will be deducted points by the assessor for poor execution.

Technical qualities

Technical qualities take into consideration **timing** and **consistency**.

- It is crucial that you are able to perform a skill at the exact moment required in order to maximise the chance of it being successful.
- Additionally, successful performance will be achievable if you can sustain a high level of performance consistently.

You can use the FACI structure to think about technical qualities. Here are two examples:

F	Physical (technical qualities)
A	Badminton
C	I need to be able to serve consistently well in badminton in order to put my opponent under pressure at the start of the rally. If I have an inconsistent serve in badminton, then I will not be able to put the shuttle where I want it to go.
I	Having poor consistency in my serve will result in the serve either going out of the court, falling short of the service line or being easily received by my opponent. If it goes out, I will lose a point.

F	Physical (technical qualities)
A	Swimming
C	As a swimmer competing in the 50 m front crawl race, it is important that I get the timing of my tumble turn correct to maintain a lead.
I	If I mistime it and tumble too early then I will be too far away and not get a strong push off the wall, which will slow my pace down. This means that my competitors could lap me and I would then be behind in the race.

Key terms

Timing The ability to perform a skill at the exact moment required to ensure a successful outcome.

Consistency The ability to produce a high level of skill execution repeatedly.

Special qualities

- Special qualities take into consideration imagination, creativity and flair.
- Having these qualities will enable you to outsmart and outwit your opponents if playing in a games context.
- If you have these qualities and are performing in an aesthetic context, these qualities will help your performance because you will be unique and original when devising your own sequence or routine.

You can use the FACI structure to think about special qualities. Here are two examples:

F	Physical (special qualities)
A	Football
C	I need creativity in football to be able to outsmart my opponent when in possession of the ball – for example, when using my skill, such as a Cruyff Turn, to take on an opponent in a 1v1 situation.
I	Taking on my opponent and being creative creates an overload in attack, which increases my team's chances of scoring.

F	Physical (special qualities)
A	Dance
C	It is important that I show good imagination when devising my dance sequence. I need to include original and complex moves that are going to make my solo performance stand out from everyone else's.
I	If I can choreograph and perform a solo that is comprised of complex and unique skills, my performance is going to be more imaginative and will be scored more highly by the judges.

Key terms

Imagination The ability to be original in your skills/ sequence selection – for example, deceiving your opponent with your shot selection in badminton.

Creativity The ability to be unique when faced with a challenge – for example, creating a unique sequence that will showcase your skill set in dance.

Flair The ability to perform a skill or technique in an exciting or interesting way – for example, having a broad range of skills that will allow you to outwit your opponent in a 1v1 situation in football.

Do you know?

1 Identify *two* different physical skills factors.
2 Describe *two* different examples of being creative in a sporting context.
3 Describe your own strengths relating to physical skills factors.
4 Describe your own development needs relating to physical skills factors.

4.2 Methods of collecting information to analyse factors impacting on performance

You need to know

- what methods you have used to collect information on physical skills
- how, when and where you carried out these methods
- why you carried out these methods
- what the benefits and limitations are of using the methods

General observation schedule

A general observation schedule provides you with a complete overview of your game because it records every shot you play.

Table 20 shows a scaled-down example.

Table 20 A general observation schedule

	Serve	Clear	Drop shot	Smash	Net play	%
Highly effective						
Fairly effective						
Ineffective						

Description of method:
- Work in a group of four.
- Two people play a game of badminton up to 21 points.
- The two people in your group who are not playing observe your game and record your shots on the sheet.
- Any time a shot is played in the game, it must be recorded as Highly effective, Fairly effective or Ineffective.
- Once the game is over, the total for each shot is added up to identify strengths and development needs.

The benefits and limitations of general observation schedules are listed in Table 21.

Table 21 The benefits and limitations of a general observation schedule

General observation schedule	
Benefits	**Limitations**
<ul><li>It gives a full overview of your whole performance.</li><li>It provides factual evidence, which is non-biased, so you obtain accurate results.</li><li>Strengths and development needs can be identified from it. You can then create a PDP and set goals to improve on it.</li><li>You can keep results as a permanent record. You can compare with future retests to check for improvements.</li></ul>	<ul><li>Results will not be accurate or reliable if the recorder lacks experience or expertise in the game.</li><li>You cannot do this independently – you are relying on working in a group.</li><li>Having an opponent who does not have similar ability to you will call the reliability of results into question.</li><li>If it is a fast-paced game, human error may come into play.</li></ul>

Scatter diagrams

A scatter diagram provides you with an overview of how accurate your shot placement is on court. Using badminton as an example, this is drawn up as follows:

Description of method:

- Work in a group of three.
- The 'feeder' feeds ten high serves to the person on the other side of the net.
- The 'performer' returns the shuttle using their weak shot, for example an overhead clear.
- The third person records on the diagram, with an X, where each shuttle lands (Figure 14).

> **Exam tip**
>
> When you are asked to analyse a method used to gather information on a factor, you should make points that look beyond the explanation. You should consider using linking terms, such as 'this means that... This will allow you to put your analytical points across well.

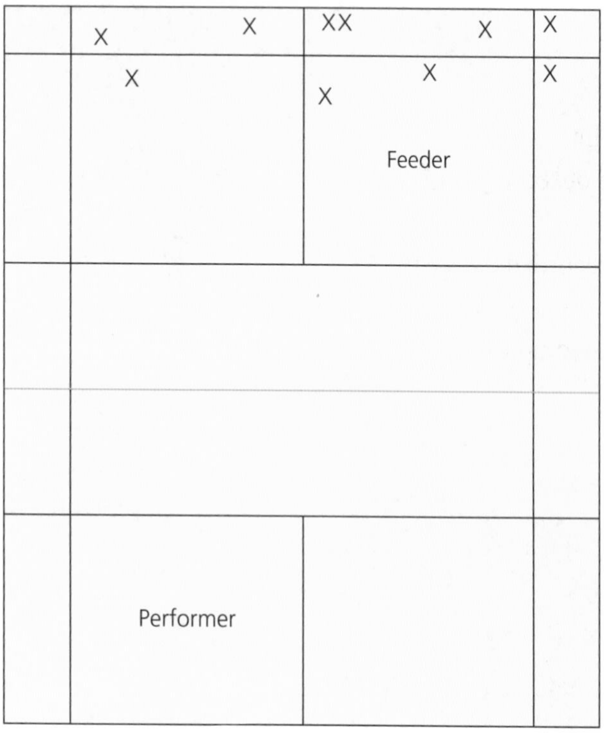

Figure 14 A scatter diagram for badminton

The benefits and limitations of scatter diagrams are listed in Table 22.

Table 22 The benefits and limitations of scatter diagrams

Scatter diagrams	
Benefits	**Limitations**
■ They give an accurate account of how effective your shot placement is. ■ They provide factual evidence, which is non-biased, so you gain accurate results. ■ You can keep results as a permanent record. You can compare with future retests to check for improvements.	■ You cannot do this independently; you are relying on working in a group of three. ■ Having an opponent who cannot provide accurate feeds will make the results unreliable.

Do you know?

1 Describe *one* method you have used to collect information on physical skills.

2 Describe a different method you have used to collect information on physical skills.

3 Explain why *one* of the methods you selected for questions 1 or 2 was appropriate.

4 Choose a method you have used to collect data on physical skills. What are the benefits and limitations of that method?

4.3 Approaches used to develop performance

You need to know
■ how to describe and explain a variety of approaches used to develop performance with regard to physical skills factors
■ how to analyse and evaluate a variety of approaches used to develop performance with regard to physical skills factors

Shadow practice

■ Shadowing involves rehearsing the movement required to perform a skill without using, for example, a ball or a shuttle.
■ Shadow practices are used to allow the performer to work out how they need to move their body in order to perform the correct technique for a skill.

- They can also be used to perform this correct movement repeatedly so that it becomes automatic.
- The amount of time spent on the drill is normally determined by working for a number of sets or repetitions, or by working and resting for set periods of time.

The benefits and limitations of shadow practice are listed in Table 23.

Table 23 **The benefits and limitations of shadow practice**

Shadow practice	
Benefits	Limitations
- The performer can concentrate on making their body complete the desired action. - With no opponents or competition the performer is not under pressure and can concentrate solely on performing the correct action. - Performers can practise at their own speed. This may mean slowing the action down to make sure that each part is being performed correctly.	- The performer can become bored if the practice is performed for too long. - Bad habits could be learned if the performer is not shadowing the correct technique. - Performers need to be highly motivated to use this type of practice regularly.

Conditioned games

To improve a skill, the normal rules of a game can be changed so that the skill being learned occurs more often or has greater importance. For example, this could include changing the number of points given when a basket is scored using a particular technique.

Any condition you want can be placed on a game. What is important when using conditioned games is that the condition allows you to continue to improve the area of the game you are focusing on. Some examples of conditions you might add include:

- more points/goals for scoring using a certain skill/technique
- only being allowed to score using a certain skill/technique
- changing the size of the playing area
- altering the number of players
- changing how points are scored

The benefits and limitations of conditioned games are listed in Table 24.

Table 24 The benefits and limitations of conditioned games

Conditioned games	
Benefits	**Limitations**
■ Performers are motivated by this approach because it involves performing in a game situation. ■ Conditions can be placed on the game that encourage the performer to use the skill/technique in a game situation. ■ The theme of the session is maintained in a competitive situation, so performers do not forget what they have been working on when they go into a game. ■ Decision-making skills can be developed in pressured situations.	■ It can be easy to forget what you are trying to develop and instead only focus on beating your opponent. ■ They can become demotivating if the practice is too difficult and you are not experiencing success.

Do you know?

1 Identify *two* approaches you have used to develop performance in relation to physical skills factors.

2 Describe *one* approach you used to develop performance in relation to physical skills factors.

3 Choose an approach. Explain why you would use this to develop performance.

4 What are the benefits and limitations of *one* approach to developing performance in relation to physical skills factors.

End of section 4 questions

1 a Describe the method(s) you could use to gather information about the impact of physical skills factors on performance.

  b Explain the appropriateness of the method(s) described in part (a).

2 Describe how you have developed physical skills factors that have impacted on performance.

3 Evaluate your strengths and development needs in comparison with a model performer in relation to physical skills factors.

4 a Describe the adaptations/changes that may need to be made when carrying out a development plan for physical fitness.

  b Explain why it might be necessary to make the adaptations/changes described in part (a).

5 Physical factors: fitness

5.1 Factors impacting on performance

You need to know
- definitions of physical fitness factors
- how physical fitness factors can impact positively or negatively on performance
- the impact of physical fitness on other factors

Cardio-respiratory endurance

- Most performers can begin a performance effectively, but overall output often drops once fatigue sets in.
- This is particularly common in sports that have prolonged periods of movement over long distances, for example swimming, rugby, football, basketball and badminton.
- Poor **cardio-respiratory endurance (CRE)** negatively affects physical performance, but it also has a huge impact on mental, emotional and social performance.

Key term

Cardio-respiratory endurance (CRE) The ability of the heart and lungs to pump oxygenated blood to the working muscles for a prolonged period.

Figure 15 highlights the potential impact of cardio-respiratory endurance on mental, emotional and social factors.

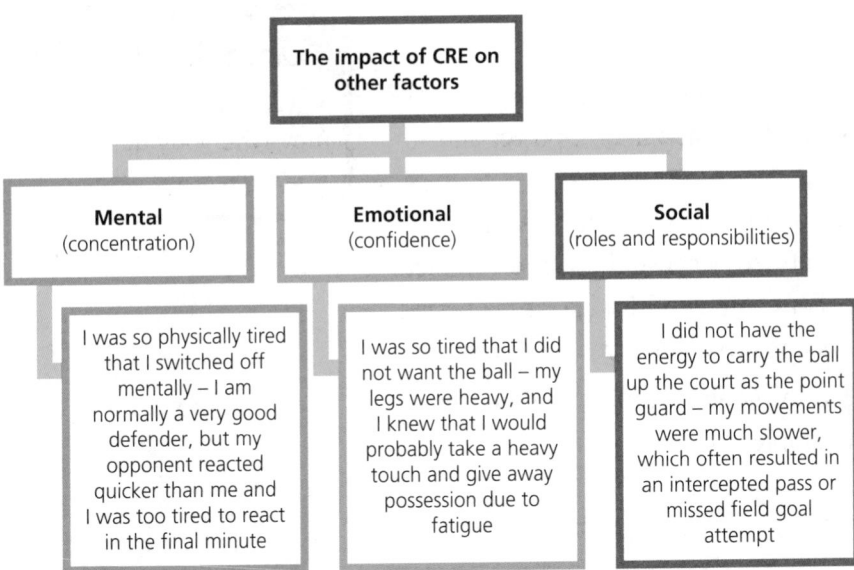

Figure 15 Examples of the impact of cardio-respiratory endurance on mental, emotional and social factors

You can use the FACI structure to think about cardio-respiratory endurance and its impact on performance. Here are two examples:

F	Physical fitness (cardio-respiratory endurance)
A	Swimming
C	Effective cardio-respiratory endurance allows me to perform at a higher standard for a longer time and therefore I am able to maintain a fast, constant pace over my 200 m freestyle. Other racers are quicker off the blocks, but I do not panic because I know I have the endurance and stroke efficiency to catch them late in the race.
I	My stroke remains long and efficient because my muscles are full of oxygenated blood. I can maintain my performance levels throughout the race and begin to chip away at their lead and power to victory as they start to fatigue in the final length.

F	Physical fitness (cardio-respiratory endurance)
A	Rugby union
C	Having poor-quality cardio-respiratory endurance means that I struggle to keep up with the pace of the game and cannot consistently make all of my tackles as we enter the last 20 minutes.
I	This results in our defensive line being broken, which often leads to us conceding late tries and losing the game. Because I am fatigued, I can also lose concentration when tackling opponents late in games. My tackle technique can suffer because of fatigue and I sometimes strike high with the shoulder, which can injure my opponent. This often leads to a penalty and a possible yellow or red card for dangerous play, which reduces my team to 14 players for at least a 10-minute spell.

Exam tip

FACI stands for Factor, Activity, Context, Impact. FACI can be applied to any factors you cover in this section.

Agility

- **Agility** is the ability to change direction quickly and precisely under control. It is a combination of speed, balance, power and coordination.
- Being agile is hugely beneficial in almost every sport. Agile performers appear much more refined because they have complete control over their movements. For example, Edin Hazard is famed for his ability to avoid tackles thanks to quick directional change.

> **Key term**
>
> **Agility** The ability to move the body quickly and precisely.

You can use the FACI structure to think about agility and its impact on performance. Here are two examples:

F	Physical fitness (agility)
A	Hockey
C	Being agile in possession allows me to turn and dribble quickly to get away from opposition defenders.
I	This allows me to maintain control of the hockey ball on both the open and reverse stick, and I can drive into open space away from opponents. Because I can evade tackles in tight areas, I am able to maintain possession for our team.

F	Physical fitness (agility)
A	Cheerleading
C	Because I struggle to change direction quickly, I often mistime steps. I can look very clumsy in my movement, lacking fluency and control.
I	I find myself behind the rest of my group and begin to panic when trying to catch up. As a base, I need to be in position to lift my flyer safely. My movements can look very rushed and unrefined, resulting in point deductions for my team.

- Agility can look very different depending on the performance context.
- Being agile allows a performer to cover distances at speed, with more fluency and efficiency.

Figure 16 highlights movements/skills from a selection of sports that require high levels of agility (speed, balance, power and coordination combined) to be performed effectively.

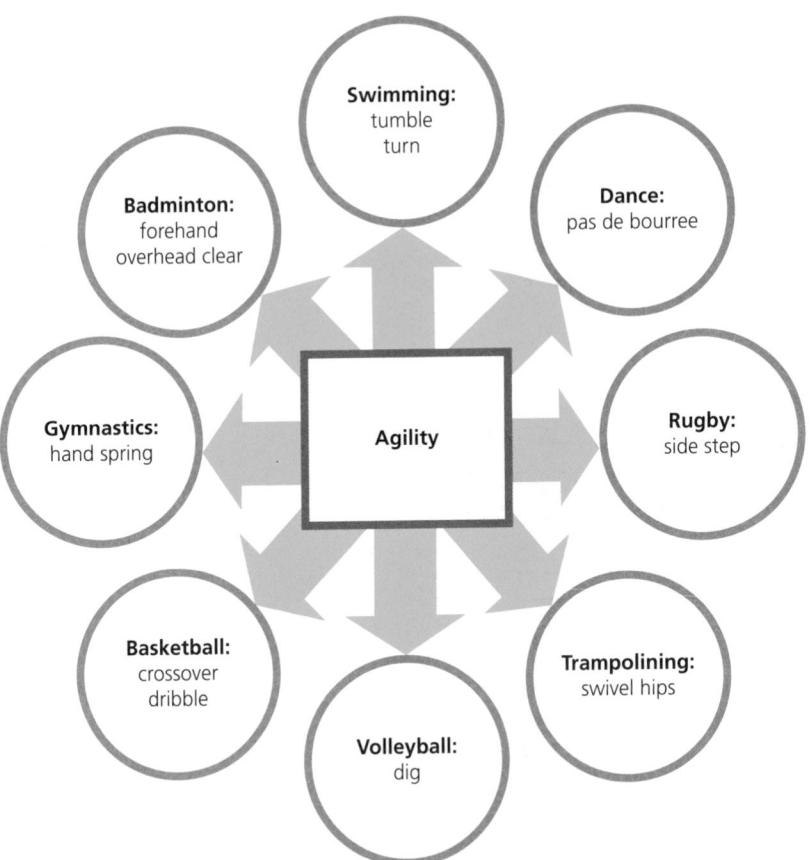

Figure 16 Examples of agility in sport

Speed

- Speed is not just about being able to run fast. It comes in various forms and can be vitally important for an effective performance.
- Speed is often divided into whole-body speed, arm speed and leg speed.

Table 25 highlights how speed can vary depending on the sport and on the body parts used.

> ### Key term
>
> Speed The ability to move all or a part of the body as quickly as possible.

Table 25 Examples of speed in sport

Sport	Body part speed	Impact on performance
Tennis	Arm speed	Increases my serve speed, making it much harder for my opponent to return. This allows me to score easy points on my serve.
Swimming	Whole-body speed	Speed in the water allows me to cut through the water faster and reduce turn time with my tumbles, resulting in improved split times.
Golf	Arm speed	A faster down swing has allowed me to strike the ball with increased speed. This has resulted in improved shot distance with my drivers and irons.
Gymnastics	Whole-body speed	A fast run-up to the vault ensures that I fully commit to my performance. If I sprint at top speed, I can generate more power off the springboard and so I have more time to execute my skill.

You can use the FACI structure to think about speed and its impact on performance. Here are two examples:

F	Physical fitness (speed)
A	Football
C	As a winger I need speed to burst past fullbacks with the ball and to chase down penetrative passes from teammates. I also need speed to make recovery runs and get back goal side quickly.
I	Being able to quickly reach penetrative passes means that I am beyond my opponent and so I have time to compose myself and pick a good pass or take on a shot, which could result in a goal. Having good speed defensively allows me to get to the ball before my opposition winger/full back, ensuring we regain possession.

F	Physical fitness (speed)
A	Badminton
C	In half-court singles, arm speed is required to play effective serves, lifts and clears. Without arm speed, I am unable to generate enough height and depth to push my opponent to the back of the court.
I	As a result of limited arm speed, the shuttle often flies to mid court, which allows my opponent to attack with a smash or drop shot, winning the point with ease.

Balance

Balance can be in two forms:

- Static balance refers to balance without movement, and is typically found in a gymnastics context. A gymnast will look to hold a balance for a prolonged period of time, highlighting to judges their supreme body control.
- Dynamic balance refers to balance with movement, and is vitally important in many sports. For example, in the pole vault the vaulter must drive their hips over their head and maintain body control and core stability over the pole to successfully clear the bar.

> **Key term**
>
> **Balance** The ability to maintain your centre of gravity over your base of support.

You can use the FACI structure to think about balance and its impact on performance. Here are two examples:

F	Physical fitness (static balance)
A	Gymnastics
C	During my floor sequence, I was able to hold all of my balances (arabesque, headstand and handstand) perfectly still for 5 seconds, and I was able to link them flawlessly into my next movement.
I	This meant that my sequence linked from start to finish and I was able to combine a variety of complex balances and fluent movements. The judges commented on my excellent control and awarded me the highest mark.

F	Physical fitness (dynamic balance)
A	Rugby
C	While taking the ball at pace I tried to sidestep my opponent. However, I was unable to maintain my centre of gravity while moving at top speed and tripped myself up.
I	On landing, I knocked the ball forward, losing possession and giving our opponents an attacking scrum.

Do you know?

1 Define *two* different physical fitness factors.

2 Describe *two* strengths or *two* areas of development in relation to physical fitness.

3 Explain how physical fitness can impact on performance.

4 Analyse the impact physical fitness can have on mental, emotional and social factors during a performance.

5.2 Methods of collecting information to analyse factors impacting on performance

You need to know

- different methods you have used to collect information for analysing how physical fitness impacts on performance
- how, when, where and why you carried these methods out
- what the benefits and limitations are of using certain methods
- how to use information gathered to plan for a personal development plan
- how and why you compare your performance to a model performance

Exam tip

When collecting data, you should look to compare your performance with a model performer. A model performer could be a classmate, teammate, teacher, coach or elite athlete.

Model performers

- Model performers exemplify quality performance.
- In a physical fitness context they will display excellent endurance, agility, speed, balance, strength etc. For example, Simone Biles is widely regarded as the best female gymnast of all time, she currently holds four Olympic gold medals. She specialises in the vault and floor – disciplines that require huge amounts of physical fitness. She has the ability to move her body at speed, with incredible control and accuracy, for a prolonged period.

Fitness testing

- Fitness testing allows a performer to gather reliable information on their physical fitness levels.
- There are many different tests that can be used to highlight specific fitness strengths and development needs.
- Every test is standardised, which means that results can be saved and compared with national norms (Table 26), providing an accurate reflection of fitness performance.

Multistage fitness run or bleep test

Description of method:

- This measures levels of cardio-respiratory endurance (CRE) and involves continuous running between two lines 20 metres apart in time with audible bleeps.
- The speed at the start is slow and builds as the performer progresses.
- The performer continues running between the two lines, turning when signalled to by the bleeps.
- If the line is reached before the bleep sounds, the performer must wait until it does before continuing.
- If the line is not reached before the bleep sounds, the performer is given a verbal warning.
- The test is stopped if the performer fails to reach the line for two consecutive ends after receiving their warning.
- The run is completed until exhaustion.

Table 26 **Comparative norms for the bleep test**

Gender	Bleep test				
	Excellent	Above average	Average	Below average	Poor
Male	>13	11–13	9–11	7–9	<7
Female	>12	10–12	8–10	6–8	<6

The benefits and limitations of fitness testing are listed in Table 27.

Table 27 **The benefits and limitations of fitness testing**

Fitness testing	
Benefits	**Limitations**
<ul><li>The tests are widely recognised and provide accurate results against standardised norms.</li><li>Each test is specific to a separate physical fitness factor.</li><li>Strengths and development needs are easily identified, and so appropriate approaches can be selected.</li><li>Results can be used to set training at an appropriate intensity.</li><li>SMART targets can be set, based on initial testing results.</li><li>Initial results can be saved and used for comparisons at a later date.</li></ul>	<ul><li>Tests are only accurate if the performer gives their very best effort.</li><li>For validity and reliability, all tests must be conducted under the same conditions for all performers.</li><li>While each test is specific to a fitness factor, it is not specific to an activity or sport. Several other factors impact on quality of performance.</li><li>Tests may require specialised equipment or measuring techniques, which could affect data reliability.</li></ul>

Observation schedules

- An observation schedule highlights the impact of fitness levels on a sporting performance.
- Typically, in terms of physical fitness, an observation schedule is completed after fitness testing has been conducted and a development need has been identified from the initial data.

CRE match analysis

- An observer completes the schedule during a performance context, hoping to identify the impact of CRE (Figure 17).
- The performance is tracked for a prolonged period to place focus on fatigue.
- Observation schedules can highlight a broad overview of performance or can be adapted to provide much more focused data.

Activity	0–10 mins	11–20 mins	21–30 mins	31–40 mins
Sprinting	/ / / / / / / / /	/ / / / /	/ / /	/
Running	/ / / / / / / / / /	/ / / / / /	/ / / /	/ /
Jogging	/ / / / /	/ / / / / / / /	/ / / / / /	/ / / /
Walking	/ /	/ / /	/ / / / /	/ / / / / /
Standing still	/ /	/ / /	/ / / / / / /	/ / / / / / / / /

Figure 17 CRE match analysis

The benefits and limitations of observation schedules are listed in Table 28.

Table 28 The benefits and limitations of observation schedules

Observation schedules	
Benefits	**Limitations**
<ul><li>Generally easy to understand and complete.</li><li>They can focus on single or multiple development areas.</li><li>The results are easy to interpret, ensuring accurate goal setting.</li><li>They clearly highlight the link between factor, impact and performance.</li><li>They can be used in conjunction with video analysis to add validity and reliability.</li></ul>	<ul><li>All performances must be competitive to ensure the athlete is challenged and the results are accurate.</li><li>The observer must understand the assessment criteria and be able to fill out information quickly.</li><li>The observer must concentrate and have some knowledge of the specific activity to truly understand the rules and demands.</li><li>Weather can cause data collection challenges, whether using paper or digital technology.</li></ul>

Exam tip

When explaining methods for gathering information, you must consider the question of 'why'. Important link words include: 'because', 'which means that', 'this allowed me to' and 'so that'. For example:

I used a CRE match analysis to measure the impact of CRE in a performance context. This was important because fitness testing alone would not be accurate enough as there would be no performance demands such as sprinting, passing, shooting, dribbling and tackling. The CRE match analysis was easy to complete and understand, which means that I could easily identify areas of development and create an appropriate development plan to improve my performance.

Do you know?

1 Describe how you have collected data on physical fitness.

2 From the data you have gathered, describe your strengths and development needs in relation to physical fitness.

3 Select *one* data collection method. Explain why you selected this method to gather data on physical fitness.

4 Explain your areas of development in relation to physical fitness.

5.3 Approaches used to develop performance

You need to know

- how to identify and carry out approaches that are appropriate for developing performance with regard to physical fitness
- how to describe a variety of approaches to develop performance with regard to physical fitness
- how to explain the use of certain approaches
- how to analyse and evaluate approaches used to develop performance with regard to physical fitness
- how to adapt or modify approaches to improve performance with regard to physical fitness

Exam tip

Consider how physical fitness (CRE, agility, speed, balance etc.) impacts positively or negatively on your performance. If you are to improve performance, you must consider your fitness levels and implement approaches that can genuinely improve your overall output.

Remember, for approaches to improve performance they must be:

- specific – to the factor you are focusing on
- realistic – in a training or performance context
- adaptable – can be simplified or overloaded to suit performance levels
- recordable – diary entries, reflections, retesting etc. – to measure the effects of the approach on performance

Fartlek training

- Fartlek is a Swedish word, which means 'speed play'.
- This approach to training can be adapted to suit running, cycling or swimming events.
- The approach is designed to mimic sport-related movements. For example, you would expect a squash player's fartlek session to vary from that of a hockey player because the game demands are very different.
- Regardless of variances, the principles remain the same – fartlek consists of short sprint bursts followed by a slower recovery, then more continuous activity
- Typically, coloured cones dictate a definite change in pace.

The benefits and limitations of fartlek training are listed in Table 29.

Key term

Overload Increasing the challenge of training once a performer has met a target or level. In a fitness context, training can be overloaded by increasing the frequency, intensity or duration of sessions/approaches. It is important to progressively overload as you improve, otherwise your performance will plateau.

Table 29 The benefits and limitations of fartlek training

Fartlek training	
Benefits	**Limitations**
<ul><li>Simple to set up and carry out, so the athlete remains engaged in training.</li><li>Easy to overload by increasing training frequency, intensity and/or duration.</li><li>Specific movement patterns are linked to many sporting performances, for example walking, jogging, running and sprinting.</li><li>Can be made more game specific by adding equipment, for example dribbling a football at varying paces.</li><li>Design can be adapted to place increased focus on, for example, CRE, speed endurance or agility.</li></ul>	<ul><li>It can become repetitious and boring over time.</li><li>While it can be made more game-specific by introducing equipment, it never truly replicates the pressure of a performance.</li><li>It only develops physical factors and therefore can be slightly one dimensional.</li><li>Requires maturity and commitment to complete effectively – often taking place in 20/30/40-minute sessions.</li></ul>

Circuit training

- Circuit training involves completing a series of exercises or activities in a structured order (see Figure 18).
- Exercises are completed to the best of the performer's ability, and are either timed (e.g. 45 seconds per station), or performed until a predetermined repetition has been achieved (e.g. 35 press-ups).
- Typically, there is an interval work-to-rest ratio (e.g. work for 60 seconds, rest for 30 seconds – 2:1).
- Stations often focus on different body parts to ensure the performer continues to work with quality throughout the session.
- Circuit training has become incredibly popular in a health and fitness context, with the likes of CrossFit, BoxFit and Functional HIIT all evolving from this concept.

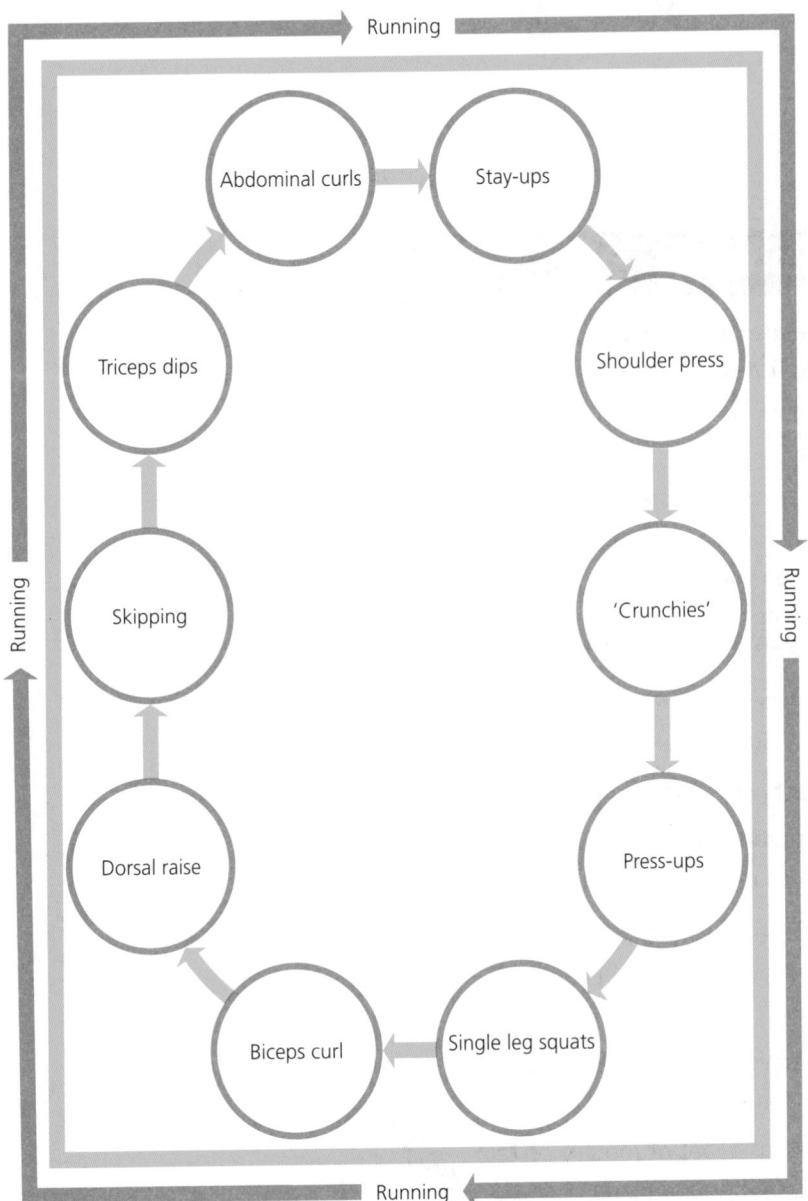

Figure 18 Typical circuit for circuit training

The benefits and limitations of circuit training are listed in Table 30.

Table 30 **The benefits and limitations of circuit training**

Circuit training	
Benefits	**Limitations**
■ Develops both general and specific fitness needs (in or out of the game). ■ The design can be adapted to place increased focus on specific physical factors, such as CRE, speed endurance, agility and balance. ■ Completed in pairs or groups, so promotes competition and quality training. ■ Can be easily overloaded by increasing sessions per week, decreasing rest intervals, increasing number of reps, or increasing circuit length. ■ Can be made more game specific by adding equipment. The skill set can be developed under fatigue.	■ Can become repetitious and boring over time. ■ Can take time to set up and execute with quality, so must be well planned. ■ Knowledge and understanding are required to ensure performers know the purpose of the approach, and how it can be adapted to suit specific fitness needs. ■ There is a danger of overtraining/ causing injury when trying to match or beat the performance of a teammate or classmate.

Do you know?

1 Describe *two* approaches you have used to develop your performance in relation to physical fitness.

2 Explain why training approaches must be based on information collected.

3 Focusing on *one* specific approach, evaluate its effectiveness in developing your performance.

4 Explain why it is important to overload sessions/approaches once a performer's fitness levels begin to improve.

End of section 5 questions

1 Describe how physical fitness impacts on performance.

2 Select *two* ways of gathering information on physical fitness. Describe how you have gathered data using these methods.

3 Analyse why *one* method might be better than the other.

4 Explain the challenges you might face when gathering data on physical fitness.

5 Describe *two* approaches that you have used to develop your performance in relation to physical fitness.

6 Explain why a performer might need to adapt or modify certain approaches during a performance development plan.

6 Physical factors: tactics

6.1 Factors impacting on performance

You need to know
- definitions of physical tactics factors
- how physical tactics can impact positively or negatively on performance
- the impact of physical tactics on other factors

Formation depth

- Football teams at all levels are placing more emphasis on possession than ever before.
- Traditional, rigid formations like 4-4-2 and 3-5-2 have been replaced by much more fluid formations such as 4-2-3-1 and 4-1-2-1-2 (see Figure 19).

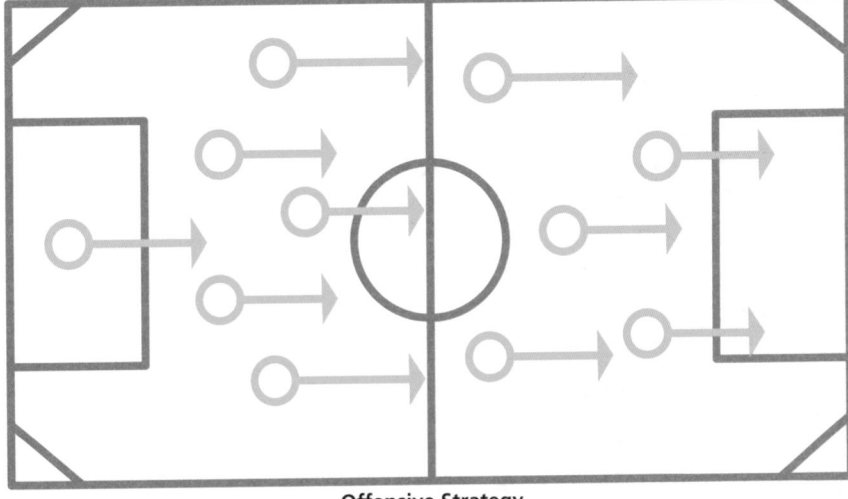

Offensive Strategy

Figure 19 Tactics board sharing a 4-1-2-1-2 formation

- In a 4-1-2-1-2 formation, the deep-lying central midfielder has a vital role to play.
- They must maintain depth and provide passing options at all times to ensure possession is maintained.
- This player also acts as a defensive guard to the back four, and allows those in more advantaged roles to freely attack the opposition.
- If one or both full backs join in with the attack, this central midfielder can deepen further and recreate a solid defensive line of four players.

You can use the FACI structure to think about formation depth and its impact on performance. Here are two examples:

F	Physical tactics (formation depth)
A	Rugby union
C	As a fullback in rugby, I need to be tactically aware in a defensive context because I am often the last line of defence. I sit deep when defending and read the game effectively so I can cover any line breaks from the opposition.
I	Because I maintain my defensive depth, I am able to cover the ground quickly, closing angles and making try-saving tackles for my team. Maintaining defensive depth also allows me to claim any loose kicks from the opposition, and I am able to scan the space ahead and either launch a counter-attack or strike a clearance kick to safety.

F	Physical tactics (formation depth)
A	Basketball
C	It is important to have an attacking structure in basketball. Our point guard needs to maintain depth as our playmaker so that we can maintain possession of the ball and make play calls in a controlled and structured manner.
I	Our point guard continued to force the play by driving towards the basket for lay-ups. She was often unsuccessful against bigger defenders, resulting in cheap turnovers. Due to our unstructured play, our point guard was no longer our first line of defence. Cheap points were often conceded through fast breaks.

Exam tip

FACI stands for Factor, Activity, Context, Impact. FACI can be applied to any factors you cover in this section.

Time of play

- Time of play refers to the stage of a race or game.
- When time is running out, for example, formation or other tactics often have to be adapted depending on the scoreline/expected outcome.

You can use the FACI structure to think about time of play and its impact on performance. Here are two examples:

F	Physical tactics (time of play)
A	Football
C	We were winning the match 1–0 in the 85th minute. However, we were under extreme pressure and could not get out of our own half because all outfield players were focused on maintaining our slender lead. We decided to bring on a second striker.
I	A second striker meant changing from a 4-5-1 formation to a 4-4-2 formation. We were able to strike passes and clearances into wide channels and he competed energetically for possession higher up the pitch. This relieved pressure on our goalkeeper and defenders and allowed us to see out the remaining minutes in our opponents' half.

F	Physical tactics (time of play)
A	800 m running
C	I was drawn in a very fast semifinal. The top three qualified automatically, as did the fastest loser. I knew I would have to run one of my best ever races, possibly sub 2 minutes, which was my personal best.
I	I started at a fast pace. If I could not make the top three, I still wanted to run a great time and qualify. Unfortunately, I could not maintain my stride length and fatigued badly in the closing stages. The pressure of needing to run a fast time affected my performance, and I lost my composure and misjudged my tactics, finishing in 6th place in a disappointing time of 2 minutes, 4 seconds.

Figure 20 highlights the potential impact of time of play on mental, emotional and social factors.

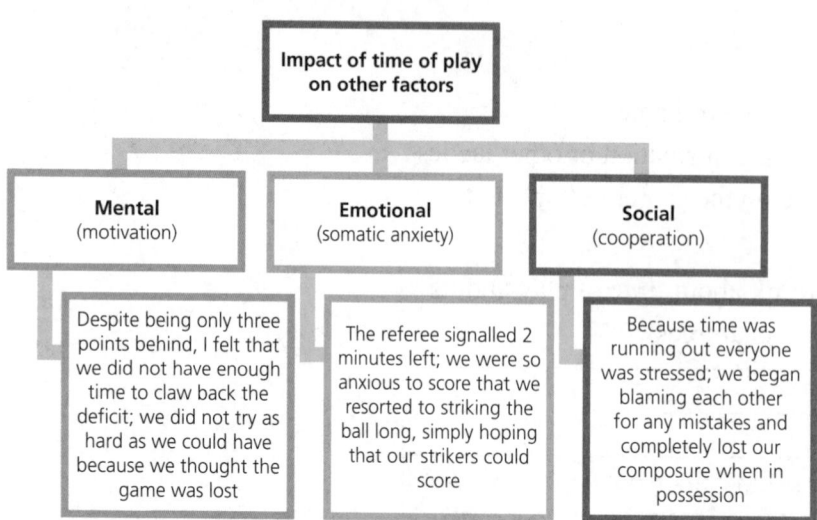

Figure 20 The impact of time of play on mental, emotional and social factors

Communication

- Communication is the ability to impart or exchange information.
- It can be verbal or non-verbal.

You can use the FACI structure to think about communication and its impact on performance. Here are two examples:

F	Physical tactics (communication)
A	Volleyball
C	As the setter, I needed to subtly communicate to my server so that our opponents are unaware of our tactics. I can make a number of subtle hand signals behind my back to indicate where my partner should serve or where I intend to block.
I	I identified a weakness in one of our opposition receivers. I hand-signalled to my server where I wanted her to serve. This resulted in a poor pick-up and I was able to block the return at the net and win an easy point.

F	Physical tactics (communication)
A	Doubles tennis
C	Our opponents returned a poor backhand to our mid-court. I was slightly off balance on my forehand side and my partner was poised to hit a backhand winner. However, neither of us called for the ball so we both played the shot and my racket struck his.
I	Due to a lack of communication, my teammate mishit his shot and struck the ball into the net, losing the point. If he had called for the ball earlier, I would have been able to leave it for him to strike.

Penetration

- Penetration is the ability to break a defensive line.
- This can be through passing, dribbling or running.

You can use the FACI structure to think about penetration and its impact on performance. Here are two examples.

F	Physical tactics (penetration)
A	Basketball
C	As a forward, I maintain my width in the outside channel before cutting towards the basket at pace, getting 'basket-side' of my marker.
I	Cutting centrally into the key allows me to receive the ball from my guard behind our opposition's defence, resulting in an opposed lay-up and easy points.

F	Physical tactics (penetration)
A	Football
C	Both of our strikers like to come short and receive the ball with their backs to goal.
I	While this was very effective for maintaining possession, we struggled to find space in midfield because our strikers were not stretching the game. If we did play penetrating passes between centre halves and full backs our strikers were never in a position to retrieve the ball. As a result, we did not create any goal-scoring opportunities and the opposition defenders were comfortable defending the spaces in front of them.

Do you know?

1 Describe *two* strengths or *two* areas of development in relation to physical tactics.

2 Describe a situation where you had to change/adapt/modify your tactics during a performance.

3 Analyse the impact that physical tactics can have on *two* other factors.

4 Evaluate the importance of playing your role within a tactical situation.

6.2 Methods of collecting information to analyse factors impacting on performance

You need to know

- different methods of collecting information to analyse the impact of physical tactics on performance
- how, when, where and why you have carried out these methods
- what the benefits and limitations are of using certain tactics
- how to use information gathered on physical tactics to plan for a personal development plan

Model performers

- Model performers exemplify quality performance.
- In a physical tactics context, a model performer will be a team player, and will provide feedback and accept it from coaches and teammates. They will also be tactically astute and have excellent positional sense in and out of possession. They will also make effective decisions based on the time of play, scoreline, strengths of opposition players, weather conditions etc. For example, Kim Little is a fantastic role model for any young performer. She is Scotland's leading goal scorer and has made well over 100 appearances for her country. Kim is regarded as one of the best central midfielders in world football. She is known for her penetrative runs from midfield and her ability to find space in the opposition penalty box. She also has excellent defensive capabilities and works with her teammates to deny space in midfield and win back possession.

Exam tip

When collecting data, you should look to compare your performance with that of a model performer. A model performer could be a classmate, teammate, teacher, coach or elite performer.

Match reports with video analysis

- Match reports are written by performers retrospectively.
- The aim is to spot strengths and areas of development in an individual's or a team's tactical performance.
- Performers must then select and implement suitable approaches to develop and improve.
- Utilising video analysis adds depth and accuracy to the match report, ensuring that performers are very clear about what they need to improve on while training.

Figure 21 is an extract from a match report, completed after the performance using video analysis to add accuracy/reliability.

Retrospective match report: basketball		Team name: Hornets Player name: J. Jones Playing position: centre
Offensive stats		
Overall points scored	15	
Field goals made/total attempts	5/11 (45.45%)	
Free throws made/total attempts	5/6 (83.33%)	
Rebounds won/total	5/16 (31.25%)	
Tactical overview of offensive performance My field goal percentage was quite low (45.45%). The video highlighted that I forced a lot of my shots from the outside – I should have played closer to the rim as a low post player. My free throw shooting was excellent (83.33%), and I was able to draw six fouls during the game. I struggled to win offensive rebounds (31.25%). Again, I needed to consider my court position and not allow defensive players to box me out with such ease.		

Figure 21 **Match report with video analysis**

The benefits and limitations of match reports with video analysis are listed in Table 31.

Table 31 **The benefits and limitations of match reports with video analysis**

Match reports with video analysis	
Benefits	**Limitations**
■ A match report builds reflection and accountability. Performers have to genuinely consider how their tactical performance impacts on their team and the opposition. Match reports inform the team's next performance. ■ The video analysis adds accuracy because performers are not reliant on memory or the subjective opinions of others. ■ The video can be slowed, paused and rewound. This allows for more in-depth analysis. ■ Being able to watch the video over and over, allows the performer to spot any patterns or inconsistencies in their performance, for example 'I struggled to maintain possession in midfield when our opponents switched to a 4-5-1 formation'.	■ A match report should be completed as soon as possible after the performance. Otherwise the process loses impact and the performer will be less focused. ■ Re-watching a performance in its entirety and completing a match report can be very time consuming. This can reduce training time. ■ Technology can fail. Batteries can die and data can be lost. ■ The reflecting player needs to have good sporting knowledge and to understand what is expected of them tactically. Only by knowing what they should do in certain situations will they be able to improve.

Opponent analysis

■ Analysing opposition tactics and individual performers now plays a key part in any preparation.

■ Being able to identify your opponents' strengths and areas of development can inform how you will approach the performance in terms of team selection or formation choice.

■ Managers or scouts will often watch an opponent the week before they are due to play each other. This provides the manager with time to fully prepare their players in a tactical context.

■ Much time is spent running through scenarios to exploit weaknesses identified in the analysis.

Table 32 Gives an example of an opponent analysis.

Table 32 **An opponent analysis from a football match**

Physical tactics	Preferred formation 4-4-2
Formation depth	No. 6, centre midfield – excellent skill set, sits deep and always provides an option to maintain possession. Very good range of passing.
Time of play	Initially played lots of short passes and had excellent movement off the ball. As the game reached 80 minutes they brought on a really physical striker and played much longer passes in a bid to score.
Communication	The goalkeeper organised the defence really well but other teammates were very quiet and some mistakes were made through miscommunication.
Penetration	No. 10 was very fast and looked to play between the centre halves. The defensive line was too high in the 85th minute and he used his speed to race clear and score the winner. It was a fantastic penetrating pass from No. 6.
Width	Both wingers (No. 7 and No. 11) played very narrow and tended to travel in field with the ball. Neither were overly fast. Our wingers should find success if we can maintain our attacking width pass with speed.

The benefits and limitations of opponent analysis are listed in Table 33.

Table 33 The benefits and limitations of opponent analysis

Opponent analysis	
Benefits	**Limitations**
▪ Provides planning focus, and allows the group time to prepare for, and adjust to, opposition strengths and areas of development. ▪ Training approaches can be adapted depending on tactical requirements. ▪ Provides detailed qualitative data on specific individuals. ▪ Can assist performers in identifying their own development needs, based upon how they perform against the opposition.	▪ The individual leading the analysis must be knowledgeable about tactics and formations. The analysis must be more than an opinion. ▪ Individuals must have the capacity to respond to such detailed information. ▪ Only analysing one performance could provide inaccurate results. ▪ Huge focus on the opposition can create an inferiority complex, and performers can overthink their tactical role, causing a distraction.

Do you know?

1 Select *one* way of gathering information on physical tactics. Describe how you have gathered data using this method.

2 From the data you have gathered, describe your strengths and development needs in relation to physical tactics.

3 Select *one* data collection method. Explain why you selected this method to gather data on physical tactics.

4 Evaluate the effectiveness of two physical tactics data collection methods.

Exam tip

If asked to describe how you collected data, consider what, how, where, when and who. For example:

> To collect data on my defensive play, I completed an overhead clear feeder drill on half a court. In week 1 of practice my partner fed me 10 shuttles high and deep to the back court. I returned them one after the other to the back tramlines. A third group member then recorded where the shuttles landed using an observation schedule to measure my accuracy.

6.3 Approaches used to develop performance

You need to know

- how to identify and carry out approaches that are appropriate for developing performance with regard to physical tactics
- how to describe a variety of approaches for developing performance with regard to physical tactics
- how to explain the use of certain approaches
- how to analyse and evaluate the approaches used to develop performance with regard to physical tactics
- how to adapt or modify the approaches used to develop performance with regard to physical tactics

Passive versus active

- Passive versus active is a gradual build-up approach that involves tapered challenges.
- Typically, the approach involves an attacking overload. In a 3v2 context, the three attackers will initially have lots of time on the ball to develop their tactical performance, while the two defenders will be completely passive – 'cold'.
- Defending players act purely as visual, physical barriers at this point.
- As attacking performers build confidence and competence, defending players become 'warm', applying some pressure to the player in possession and their active teammates.
- The defending players will not actively intercept the ball at this point. Once quality and consistency have been established, defending players become 'hot' and look to apply game-like pressure to intercept and turnover possession.

The benefits and limitations of the passive versus active approach are listed in Table 34.

Table 34 The benefits and limitations of the passive versus active approach

Passive versus active	
Benefits	**Limitations**
■ Limited pressure ensures that the players in possession get more time to scan their options and can decide when you move, pass, dribble or shoot with more confidence. ■ Pressure can be increased gradually as the attacking players become more confident with their tactical/technical roles. Defending players can transition from 'cold' to 'warm' to 'hot' defence to add challenge. ■ New in-play tactics and specialised set plays can be practised and perfected under varying degrees of pressure. ■ Conditions can be placed on individuals to add challenge or promote inclusion.	■ Can create a false sense of game tempo. Attacking players can become complacent, assuming they will have that time and space in a match scenario. ■ Defensive players can become frustrated and uninterested when the conditions mean that they cannot commit as they normally would.

Exam tip

Consider how physical tactics (formation depth, time of play, communication, penetration etc.) impact positively or negatively on your performance. If you are to improve performance, you must consider your tactical awareness and implement approaches that can genuinely improve your overall output.

Remember, that for approaches to improve performance they must be:
● specific – to your factor focus
● realistic – in a training or performance context
● adaptable – can be simplified or overloaded to suit performance levels
● recordable – diary entries, reflections, retesting etc. can measure the effect of an approach on performance

Conditioned games

- Conditioned games come in a variety of forms.
- The games are constructed to ensure that individuals work on specific development needs.
- Conditioned games place focus on certain factors by adapting rules and regulations.
- Depending on performance context, conditioned games could mean a change to pitch dimensions, scoring systems, equipment types, playing numbers, time in possession etc.
- Games should have a personalised feel and every performer should be challenged and included.
- Within the same game of conditioned futsal, one performer could be on a condition of two-touch, another performer might be on a condition of left-foot shooting only, while a third performer may be a floater, who the defensive team must attempt to mark to prevent an attacking overload.

The benefits and limitations of conditioned games are listed in Table 35.

Table 35 **The benefits and limitations of conditioned games**

Conditioned games	
Benefits	**Limitations**
■ Multiple factors can be developed in a game context, for example physical fitness, physical skills and physical tactics. ■ Development is more comprehensive because performers will also be developing their decision making, problem solving, resilience, communication etc. in a game context. ■ Tactics can be practised in a realistic game-like scenario, with controlled levels of pressure. ■ A variety of conditions can be placed on individual performers to add challenge or promote inclusion.	■ A high level of knowledge is required to ensure that the game is challenging and set at the appropriate level for all performers. Differentiation strategies are vitally important. ■ Individuals might have varying conditions placed on them, depending on the quality of their performance. This can be difficult to track.

Exam tip

If asked to evaluate an approach you must provide a judgement and value. For example:

> My conditioned game session was a perfect length. I trained for 30 minutes rather than 45 minutes. The shorter session allowed me to train at a higher intensity and kept me focused, so boredom did not become a factor. Because I was focused for the full session, my performance levels were much higher and my performance improved.

Do you know?

1 Describe *two* approaches that you have used to develop your performance with regard to physical tactics.
2 Explain why you selected these approaches to develop your performance.
3 Explain why a performer may need to adapt or modify certain approaches during a performance development plan.
4 Describe the impact your approaches have had on your overall performance.

End of section 6 questions

1 Explain how physical tactics can impact on performance.
2 Describe *two* methods used to collect information on the impact of physical tactics on performance.
3 Evaluate your tactical strengths and development needs in comparison with a model performer.
4 Select *one* data collection method. Explain why you selected this method to gather data on physical tactics.
5 Evaluate the overall effectiveness of approaches used to develop your performance with regard to physical tactics.

7 Performance development process

7.1 Purpose of specific performance development planning

You need to know

- the importance of making your personal development plan specific to your current performance level within an activity
- the relevant principles of effective practice when devising a personal development plan
- the relevant principles of training when devising a personal development plan

Stages of skill learning

When devising a personal development plan, performers need to ensure that practices are at the correct stage so that improvements can be made. The three stages are outlined below.

Cognitive stage (planning)

At this stage the performer is gathering information on what to do and how to do it. Most of the information is gathered through visual demonstration and verbal instruction. During this stage it is important to remember the following:

- The performer will make many mistakes and the action will lack control and refinement.
- The performer will also be reliant on lots of instructions and feedback, so feedback must be accurate and precise in order to improve its effectiveness.
- Practice sessions will be short in duration in order to avoid boredom but long enough for meaningful progress to be made.

Exam tip

When at the cognitive stage of skill learning, shadow practice would be a relevant and appropriate approach. Shadow practice allows performers to mimic the action of the skill repeatedly (without any external pressures) until they groove the correct technique.

Associative stage (practice)

At this stage the performer is putting the movements together. Practices will allow the performer to become familiar with the sequence and timing of the various parts (subroutines) involved. During this stage it is important to remember the following:

- The performer will begin to correct small faults, then repeat the corrected movements over and over again (repetition).
- The performer still has to think about the execution of the skill, but some parts will become automatic (the skill is starting to become grooved in their motor memory).
- The performer can now execute the skill in more demanding performance situations and practices, but the skill can still break down under moderate pressure.
- Performers are still reliant on instruction and feedback to reinforce various subroutines when performing the movements. However, they should be starting to rely more on internal feedback (kinaesthetic).

Autonomous stage (automatic)

At this stage most key subroutines have become automatic to the performer. As a result, little attention is paid to performing the skills, so performers can select the skill and perform it to a high standard. During this stage it is important to remember the following:

- The performer's higher skill level means that errors are less likely and the performance is consistently good.
- Performers can devote more attention to more detailed aspects of the performance, such as tactical considerations.
- Performers are capable of identifying their own errors and correcting them themselves without needing additional feedback from others.
- The key role of the teacher at this level is to assist with finer details of technique or focusing on strategy or mental preparation.

Principles of effective practice

Before carrying out a personal development plan, it is important that the approaches performers use are relevant and appropriate. Therefore, performers need to take into consideration the principles of effective practice listed in Table 36.

> **Exam tip**
>
> When at the associative stage of skill learning, repetition practice would be a relevant and appropriate approach. Repetition practice allows performers to repeat a particular skill exactly the same way over and over again. This approach eliminates the distraction of the game and other skills.

> **Exam tip**
>
> When at the autonomous stage of skill learning, conditioned games would be a relevant and appropriate approach. Conditioned games allow performers to practise chosen skills in a competitive game situation. As skills are developed in a competitive situation, performers do not simply forget what they have been working on during the session when they go into a game.

> **Exam tip**
>
> The acronym 'SMARTERVP' will help you to remember the principles of effective practice described in Table 35.

Table 36 Principles of effective practice

Specific	Practice must be specific to the performer's ability (not too difficult or too easy) and their experience in the activity. It must also relate to the results of analysis and the type of skill (open/closed) the performer is trying to develop. Finally, it must also relate to the stage of skill learning the performer is at.
Measurable	Performers should set measurable targets for improvements. This can be done through carrying out a method of collecting information and then retesting with the same method every three weeks to check for improvements. Practices should show success and achievement.
Achievable	Practice should be challenging yet achievable in order to allow for success and keep levels of motivation high. Repeating a practice over and over will eventually groove the action into the performer's muscle memory. Once this has been achieved performers can progress on to the next level.
Realistic	Practice must be realistic to the challenges of the game (game-like). By doing this it is easier to transfer a performer's improvements back into the activity, slowly increasing the pressures and making it more game-like when the performer is ready.
Timed	Adequate time (work-to-rest ratio) should be allowed for the performer to improve their skill. If the session is too short, learning will be reduced; if too long, fatigue and boredom will set in, which could lower the skill level. Practices must have intervals of rest to maintain quality. This will avoid fatigue setting in and increase motivation. Regular practice is required to ensure learning takes place – a minimum of two to three sessions per week.
Exciting	Practice must be exciting and challenging. This makes performers want to practise and keeps high levels of motivation and concentration. A short, exciting and interesting training session is better than a long session in which performers become bored and uninterested.
Recorded	Performers should make a record of what their training goals are in their training diary. As they achieve their short-term goals, they should make a record of that too. This keeps focus and also allows performers to keep track of progress.
Variation	Practice must be varied so that performers are motivated to improve and learn the skill in different situations. This also prevents boredom.
Progression	Practice must show progression. To develop a skill, performers can move on to increasingly demanding practice. This could be by increasing the level of competition, performing the skill in a shorter time period, increasing the level of accuracy required by the skill, performing the skill repeatedly over a long period of time and being able to cope with the subsequent demands.

Principles of training

Performers need to take into consideration principles of training when creating a plan of work to ensure that improvement in performance occurs.

> **Exam tip**
>
> The acronym 'SPORT' will help you to remember principles of training (Table 37).

Table 37 The principles of training

Specificity	Performers must ensure training is specific to the activity, to the area of development and to the performer's current level of fitness.
Progressive Overload	This principle should be applied as performers progress through their personal development plan. Overload should be applied only when the performer is ready to make their personal development plan more challenging. If progression occurs too soon, performers may plateau or be at risk of injury.
Reversibility	Performers should avoid taking extended breaks when undertaking their six-week personal development plan, otherwise reversibility will set in. As the saying goes, 'use it, or lose it'.
Tedium	In order to remain motivated, performers should ensure that they avoid tedium within their personal development plan. This can be done by using a variety of approaches to keep them interested.

Do you know?

1 Identify the *three* stages of skill learning.

2 Describe the principles of training a performer might take into consideration when planning a personal development plan.

3 Explain what a performer might consider before carrying out a personal development plan.

4 Explain *four* reasons why a performer might consider principles of effective practice when carrying out a personal development plan with regard to physical factors.

7.2 How to create and implement a personal development plan

You need to know

- what development needs have been identified
- how to explore approaches to address the development needs
- how to plan and implement a personal development plan
- the importance of adapting and modifying PDPs while developing performance

What is a personal development plan?

- Throughout the Higher Physical Education course you will collect data on all four factors impacting on performance (mental, emotional, social and physical).
- You will then be tasked with planning, undertaking and reviewing your own personal development plan.
- This plan should be specific to your personal needs and the sport in which you perform.
- The purpose of the plan is to genuinely improve your overall performance.
- Within a Higher Physical Education class each plan should differ. For example, based on data collection results, student A may be looking to develop their CRE and decision making, while student B may be looking to develop their agility and shot control.

What to consider when creating a personal development plan

When planning your personal development plan there are many things that need to be considered to ensure that the selected approaches are appropriate for you:

- Is the approach suitable for my level of fitness, stage of skill learning, activity experience etc.?
- Does the approach link specifically to my sport, playing position and performance context?
- Have I given the approach enough time to take effect?
- Does the approach specifically target my area of development?
- Can the approach be adapted or modified if improvements are quick or indeed nonexistent?
- Is the approach practical? Is it easy to set up, easy to overload, feasible in varying weather conditions/facilities?
- Can progression be recorded and monitored to measure improvement?

Figure 22 simplifies the personal development plan process and provides key information within the planning, doing and reviewing stages.

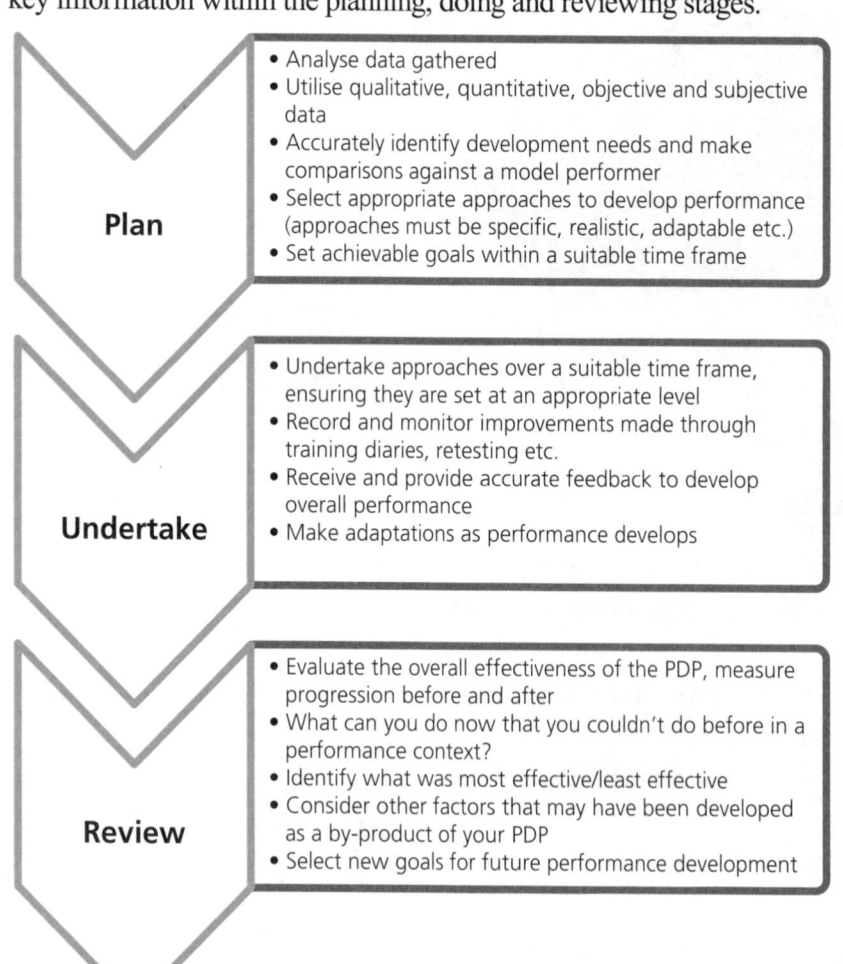

Plan
- Analyse data gathered
- Utilise qualitative, quantitative, objective and subjective data
- Accurately identify development needs and make comparisons against a model performer
- Select appropriate approaches to develop performance (approaches must be specific, realistic, adaptable etc.)
- Set achievable goals within a suitable time frame

Undertake
- Undertake approaches over a suitable time frame, ensuring they are set at an appropriate level
- Record and monitor improvements made through training diaries, retesting etc.
- Receive and provide accurate feedback to develop overall performance
- Make adaptations as performance develops

Review
- Evaluate the overall effectiveness of the PDP, measure progression before and after
- What can you do now that you couldn't do before in a performance context?
- Identify what was most effective/least effective
- Consider other factors that may have been developed as a by-product of your PDP
- Select new goals for future performance development

Figure 22 Creating a personal development plan

Planning

- Planning is vitally important within your personal development plan.
- The data you gather must be stored for future comparisons and used to accurately create your personal development plan.
- The data you store also allow you to set very clear and realistic goals to work towards. Questionnaires, match reports, video analysis, standardised testing, observation schedules and profiling wheels are just some examples of initial data collection methods that can be repeated over time.

When comparing data to monitor and evaluate your progression, you must consider the following:

- What has improved?
- Can I provide qualitative and/or quantitative evidence of improvements made?
- Has anything regressed/weakened?
- What might be the reason(s) for regression?
- What has been the impact on my overall performance?

Goal setting

Setting realistic goals has many benefits. For example:

- It motivates performers.
- It improves cohesion.
- It increases confidence.

> **Exam tip**
>
> Short-term goals can be for a training session about to take place, a training game next week or a tournament in a couple of weeks. These goals tend to change or evolve on a regular basis, and will reflect the immediate improvements in a performance. They should provide stepping-stones that will help a performer achieve their long-term goal.

Effective goal setting should be based on SMART principles:

S	Specific to what it is you are trying to achieve.
M	Measurable, in that a starting point or level is established that can be compared with the finishing level.
A	Achievable for the performer, in that the target is not too easy or too difficult.
R	Recorded in a format that will allow for accurate performance development monitoring.
T	Time set for when training is to be completed.

> **Exam tip**
>
> If asked to evaluate the effectiveness of your personal development plan you must consider the usefulness and appropriateness of approaches used. You must also consider the most effective/least effective elements of the process.
>
> If asked to evaluate your performance having completed your personal development plan, you must consider improvements made in a performance context. You must also consider whether your development needs have truly improved or if there is still work to be done.

> **Exam tip**
>
> What to consider when setting goals:
> - The intention of the goal must be made clear.
> - To distinguish between short- and long-term goals you must mention the time/duration required to achieve this goal.

> **Exam tip**
>
> Long-term goals are achieved over a prolonged period of time. For example, you may want to achieve your long-term goal by the end of the season.

When setting goals to develop performance, you should consider:

- current level of performance
- timeline for the factor to improve
- the ability to monitor progress towards achieving goals
- competition phases
- how goals are used – to enhance motivation/focus
- a model/skilled performer
- approaches for meeting the goal

Do you know?

1 Describe your personal development plan for *one* factor (mental, emotional, social or physical).

2 Describe your personal development plan for a different factor.

3 Explain what a performer might need to consider when setting goals.

4 Evaluate your performance in one factor, having completed your personal development plan.

End of section 7 questions

1 Identify the three stages of skill learning.

2 Choose a factor. Explain the principles of effective practice you took into consideration when planning your PDP.

3 Choose a factor. Explain the principles of training you took into consideration when planning your PDP.

4 Explain the principles you applied as you progressed through a PDP in the physical factor.

5 Describe one short-term goal and one long-term goal you set when developing the emotional factor.

8 Monitoring and evaluating performance development

8.1 Monitoring performance development

You need to know
- how to monitor performance in relation to the performance development process
- the importance of monitoring in relation to the performance development process

Method to monitor: training diary

- Training diaries are incredibly useful for recording, **monitoring** and evaluating performance development.
- They allow performers to gather detailed qualitative data on thoughts and feelings towards approach quality, session frequency, intensity, duration, progress being made etc.
- Diaries also allow performers to gather a host of quantitative data, such as match results, points won on serve, distance covered and turnovers won.
- If completed effectively, diaries can produce some excellent information. They help performers to set, achieve and reset targets/goals.

Key term

Monitoring The regular checking of progress over time. If no or limited progress is noted the performer can then make adaptations to the approaches used. If clear progress is being made, the performer can set new development targets and goals. Having clear targets to work towards ensures that the performer remains motivated.

Exam tip

Monitoring methods can also be used to evaluate overall progress. The key differential is when the recording was carried out. For example, a training diary that is carried out in weeks 1, 3, 5 and 7 is a monitoring tool because it is checking for progress over a prolonged period of time, and can be used to inform the performer about the effectiveness of approaches used.

When using a training diary, you should make notes on the following information:

- How you felt before the match/performance started – excited/anxious.
- If it was a game, what was the result?
- What went well in the game/performance?
- What did you identify that needs improving?
- Specific feedback that was given to you from peers/coach.
- How specific factors impacted on your performance.

Figure 23 shows how improvement should be analysed.

Figure 23 Analysing performance

Method to monitor: feedback

Feedback is an essential part of learning. As feedback is received, a performer can gauge what needs to change or remain the same about their performance.

Feedback can be **intrinsic** (feedback from yourself) or **extrinsic** (feedback from others).

There are five types of feedback (Table 38).

Table 38 Types of feedback

Type	Definition	Example	Benefits	Limitations
Kinaesthetic	The physical feel of a performance as it is being performed	I can feel my arms were bent in my handstand	You know instantly if you have performed it well or not	You may have a clouded view of yourself and be more critical than necessary
Verbal	Spoken guidance from someone (teacher, coach, peer) on how you are doing	Listening to someone giving instructions	Helps to explain a visual image and provides the performer with information on how to improve	Can be time consuming and may cause information overload
Visual	Involves the performer being able to see something	A demonstration, photo, video, YouTube clip etc.	Creates a visual image because the performer can see what is expected	Important that the demonstration is clear and correct, or it will be ineffective
Written	Written notes detailing how well you are doing and what to improve	I was given two pink sticky notes with positives from my performance	Can be kept as a permanent record and compared with future feedback to check for improvements	May become misplaced and the information might not be remembered
Knowledge of results	Being given results at the end of a performance	I scored 10/15 attempted lay-ups	Provides you with factual evidence on how you are doing	It only provides data; it does not give specific information on where a weakness lies

---

Exam tip

Training diaries can be adapted and modified to monitor/evaluate all factors impacting on performance – mental, emotional, social and physical.

Key terms

Intrinsic feedback
Feedback from within, requiring the ability to self-correct a performance. This often occurs kinaesthetically – elite performers can feel if a particular skill/movement/performance was effective or ineffective and can adapt and improve almost immediately.

Extrinsic feedback
Feedback from others, requiring the ability to take on board advice from an external source, typically a teacher, coach, manager, teammate or classmate.

Importance of monitoring performance

■ It allows you to track your progress to see if you have improved. This allows you to identify whether your development plan is on track to be successful and effective in helping you to improve.

■ Monitoring your performance development can provide you with encouragement to keep training to achieve your goals. It can be motivational, especially when you are succeeding, because it makes you want to continue to improve, knowing that you are doing well.

■ Monitoring performance development can show where progress has been made throughout the development plan or highlight where there is need for more development. You can then make the relevant changes or adaptations to your plan to ensure that you will keep improving.

■ You can compare performances to show if progress has been made and highlight further areas for development. This can be motivational, especially when you are succeeding, because you want to continue to improve.

■ Training can then be altered to ensure smooth progression. For example, if improvements are noted, training can be made more difficult to take this into account. If no checks are made, time could be wasted on practices that are either too difficult or too easy.

Exam tip

Remember ... For feedback to have positive impact it must be ...

■ immediate
■ positive
■ accurate
■ specific to the individual
■ concise and easy to act upon

Quality feedback in any form helps performers to set, achieve and reset targets/goals.

Do you know?

1 Analyse the benefits and limitations of the different types of feedback.

2 Explain whether the feedback you received during your PDP was useful or not.

3 Describe how you monitored your progression in relation to *one* factor of your choice.

4 Explain why it is necessary to monitor your performance development.

8.2 Evaluating performance development

You need to know

- what methods are appropriate for evaluating performance development
- how to evaluate performance in relation to the performance development process

Why is it important to evaluate performance?

- Evaluating your plan and the data you collected on your performance is important. It allows you to look at the information gathered and determine whether the approaches used impacted on your performance. The evaluation process is systematic and objective.
- Retesting allows the performer to check for improvements. In the example below, the performer is retesting to check for physical fitness improvement, more specifically in relation to cardio respiratory endurance (CRE).
- Retest results help performers to set, achieve and reset targets/ goals based on scores achieved.

For validity and reliability, it is vitally important that retesting is completed under the exact conditions as initial testing. For example, when retesting the bleep test, running surfaces must be the same, running distance must be exact and footwear must be consistent. Tables 39–41 show an example.

Table 39 Example of consistent conditions for the bleep test

Initial test conditions, pre PDP	Retest conditions, week 4
Indoor sports hall, wooden surface, 22 degrees	Indoor sports hall, wooden surface, 24 degrees
20 metres measured exactly by trundle wheel	20 metres measured exactly by trundle wheel
Indoor trainers, ideal for sports hall	Indoor trainers, ideal for sports hall

Table 40 **Bleep test standards**

Gender	Excellent	Above average	Average	Below average	Poor
Male	>13	11–13	9–11	7–9	<7
Female	>12	10–12	8–10	6–8	<6

Table 41 **Example bleep test results**

Initial test	Mid-point retest (week 4)	End-point retest (week 8)
Level 9.9 (average)	Level 10.4 (average)	Level 11.1 (above average)

Exam tip

Remember that fitness testing and retesting will highlight improvements in general fitness levels, but more in-depth match/performance analysis is often required to measure activity-specific improvements.

Do you know?

1 Identify *one* method that is appropriate for evaluating performance development.
2 Describe *one* method that you have used to evaluate your personal development plan.
3 Explain why the method chosen in question 2 was appropriate.

8.3 Identifying future development needs

You need to know
- how to maintain and improve your current performance levels
- how to identify your next steps for future performance development
- how to use the cycle of analysis to develop different factors impacting on performance

Throughout your Higher PE course, you will have completed the cycle of analysis (Figure 24).

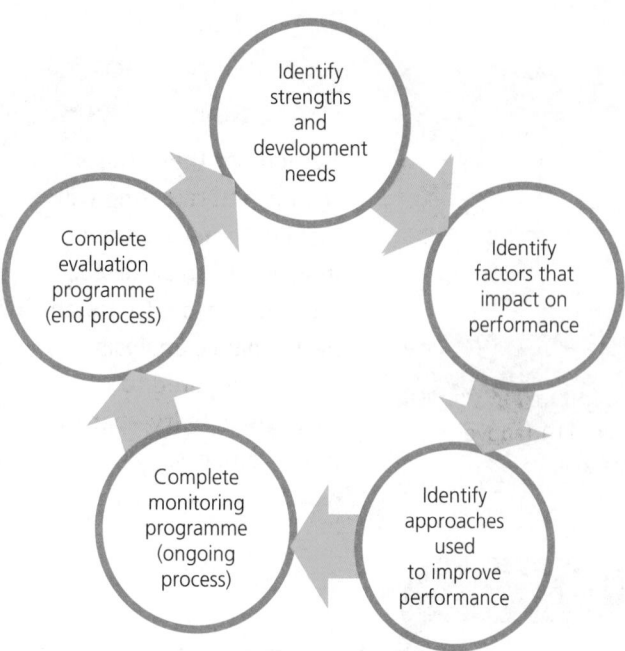

Figure 24 Cycle of analysis

Once you have completed the cycle, it is important to focus your attention on the next stage of your performance review, which is to identify future development needs. Identifying your future needs will be based on all the information you have gathered on your performance – the data collection/monitoring programme.

Your future development needs could include any of the following:
- Continue to develop existing needs.
- Improve social team dynamics and communication with teammates.
- Improve mental concentration throughout the game.
- Improve decision making in sporting contexts.
- Improve skill level, to put pressure on opponents during a performance.
- Improve fitness level to ensure a sustained, effective performance throughout the game.
- Improve overall understanding of roles and responsibilities within the game.
- Improve ability to control aggression in a challenging context.

Do you know?

1 Identify *two* future development needs in a factor of your choice.
2 Describe your *two* development needs in relation to your chosen factor in question **1**.
3 Explain why you have identified the future development needs in question **1**.
4 Evaluate the overall effectiveness of your PDP and highlight your next steps.

End of section 8 questions

1 a i Describe *one* method used to monitor the impact of *emotional factors* on performance development.

   ii Describe a different method used to evaluate the impact of *emotional factors* on performance development.

   b Explain why you would select the methods described in part (a).

2 Explain the importance of monitoring when developing *physical factors* that impact on performance.

3 Explain what you consider to now be a development need(s) with regard to *physical factors*.

4 Explain the importance of receiving quality feedback when developing *social factors* that impact on performance.

5 Analyse the method(s) you could use to monitor the development of *mental factors* that impact on performance.

6 Explain the importance of reviewing progress at the end of a performance development plan with regard to *mental factors*.

7 Explain what a performer might consider important when planning and carrying out a performance development plan on *physical factors*.